A2 Pre-intermediate

Listening

Chris Flint & Jamie Flockhart

Collins

HarperCollins Publishers
The News Building
1 London Bridge Street
London SE1 9GF

First edition 2013

10 9 8 7 6 5 4 3 2

© HarperCollins Publishers 2013

ISBN 978-0-00-749775-1

Collins® is a registered trademark of
HarperCollins Publishers Limited.

www.collinselt.com

A catalogue record for this book is available
from the British Library.

Typeset in India by Aptara

Printed by CPI Group (UK) Ltd, Croydon, CR0 4YY

About the authors

Chris Flint has been involved in language teaching for the past 20 years – as a teacher, editor and writer. He has taught students of all ages and levels in the UK and Spain, and has written various course books, online courses and a range of supplementary materials for adults and young learners.

Jamie Flockhart is a lexicographer and ELT author based in the UK. He taught English in Europe and Asia for several years before going on to work in dictionary and ELT publishing. He has since worked on a broad variety of English language learning materials, including General English and Business English books, and learner dictionaries. Jamie is co-author of *Business Vocabulary in Practice* (Collins, 2012) and *Work on your Phrasal Verbs* (Collins, 2012).

CONTENTS

INTRODUCTION

Collins English for Life: Listening will help you to improve your understanding of English and develop your listening skills. Using the book and CD will help you develop:

- listening for general understanding
- listening for specific details or information
- awareness of clear usage and structures
- your range of everyday English vocabulary
- cultural awareness

Who is this book for?

Collins English for Life: Listening is suitable for:

- elementary to intermediate learners
- learners who are CEF (Common European Framework) level A2+.

You can use *Listening*

- as a self-study course
- as supplementary material on a general English course.

Using *Listening*

Listening comprises a **book** and **CD**. The **book** consists of 20 units, divided into the following sections:

1 Who are you?
2 Where do you live?

3 What do you do?
4 What do you enjoy?

You can either work through the units from Unit 1 to Unit 20 or pick and choose the units that are most useful to you.

At the back of the book are the following useful documents:

- a mini-dictionary
- the answer key
- the transcripts for the audio recordings

The mini-dictionary lets you look up unfamiliar words and phrases. It contains definitions and examples from Collins COBUILD dictionaries. The audio transcripts highlight words or phrases that feature in the mini-dictionary with an <u>underline</u>.

Using the CD

This icon indicates that there is an audio track that you should listen to on the CD. Please note that the *Listening* CD is designed for use on a computer. If you want to play the audio on a CD player, you should download the tracks to a computer and then burn the tracks you require onto a CD.

Some of the recordings will be difficult to understand at first, but the task will be to follow the main ideas expressed and to familiarize yourself with unfamiliar ways of speaking English.

Unit structure

Getting started

Each unit begins with a few simple questions to introduce the topic and to help you prepare for the recordings and exercises which follow.

Exercises

Each unit is organized into several parts (A, B, C, etc.) with an audio track number to show you which recording to listen to. Exercises (1, 2, 3, etc.) progress from a basic check of your general understanding through to a more in-depth check of more detailed information. Working through exercises in this book will allow you to:

- **use** photos or graphics to help you understand what you are listening to
- **answer** simple questions to check your understanding of what is said
- **decide** if statements are true or false
- **choose** from multiple-choice answers
- **fill in** gaps to increase your awareness of particular language areas
- **match** words and phrases with similar meanings to widen your vocabulary
- **complete** tables with information based on what you hear

Features

In addition to the exercises, each unit contains several features to provide useful information relating to what you hear in the recordings. These are:

Clear usage

These sections focus on specific words, phrases, or grammar forms used by the speakers in the audio recordings. These are clearly explained in order to help you use the words and forms correctly and understand them better when you hear them.

Useful vocabulary and phrases

These sections highlight key words and phrases that relate to the unit topic. The words or phrases are often used in the audio recordings, but extra material may also be included here to help you improve your English vocabulary.

Listening tip

These offer tips and advice to help you improve your listening skills. Tips may help you complete an exercise or develop your awareness of different features of spoken English.

Speech bubbles

Sections set in speech bubbles highlight and give the meanings of words or phrases that may be unfamiliar to learners of English. These may include regional or more informal expressions.

COBUILD check

To help you understand and improve your vocabulary, key words or phrases from the recordings are presented, with definitions and examples from Collins COBUILD dictionaries and the COBUILD corpus.

My review

At the end of each unit you will find a checklist of the main listening skills covered in the unit. This helps you to keep track of which skills you have learned.

Other titles

Also available in the *Collins English for Life* series at A2 level: *Speaking*, *Reading*, and *Writing*.

Also available in the *Collins English for Life* series at B1 level: *Listening*, *Speaking*, *Reading*, and *Writing*.

1 FAMILY LIFE

Getting started

1 Do you have brothers and sisters?
2 Who is the oldest and youngest in your family?
3 Where does your family live?
4 Do you have similar or very different personalities?

Part A

In this recording, you will hear six people answer the questions 'Do you have brothers and sisters?' and 'Who is the oldest and youngest in your family?'

01

Look at the pictures. Circle the person who is speaking.

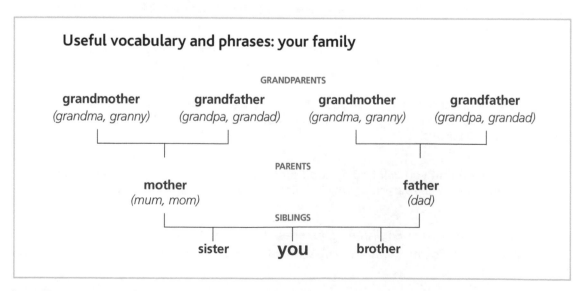

Useful vocabulary and phrases: your family

GRANDPARENTS

grandmother   **grandfather**   **grandmother**   **grandfather**
(grandma, granny)   (grandpa, grandad)   (grandma, granny)   (grandpa, grandad)

PARENTS

mother   **father**
(mum, mom)   (dad)

SIBLINGS

sister   **you**   brother

Part B

In this recording, Andrew, the twin brother from Section A talks about where his brother and sisters live and how often they meet up. Andrew lives in London.

02

1 Listen to the recording. Add arrows to show where Andrew's brother and sisters live in England on the map.

© Colllins Bartholomew Ltd 2012

Clear usage: 'try and' + (verb)

Andrew says:

'we *try and* meet up when we can'
'we *try and* make excuses to meet up'

Putting *try and* before a verb means you want to do something, and you make an effort to do it – Andrew and his family make an effort to meet up.

You may also hear *try to* + (verb), which means exactly the same thing.

---

2 Read the questions first, then play the recording. The questions check your general understanding. Circle the correct answers.

1 Which brother or sister lives closest?

  a his brother **b** his older sister **c** his twin sister

2 Which brother or sister lives furthest away?

  a his brother **b** his older sister **c** his twin sister

3 When do they meet up?

  a once a year **b** in the holidays **c** all the time

4 What do all the brothers and sisters like?

  a food **b** music **c** sports

5 Why do they meet up?

  a to travel **b** because they want to **c** for sports competitions

---

Listening tip: hearing repeated words

Andrew often repeats words. He says 'play tennis *or or* squash'. Don't be distracted by this. Repeating words is natural and helps the speaker to stop and think. Repeated words are often small, like articles (*a, an, the*), pronouns (*we, she*), and conjunctions (*but, and, or*).

Listen again carefully to Andrew. Complete the gaps in what Andrew says with the words / phrases in the box.

make excuses	several hours away	close
in particular	as well	holiday times

1 I live quite .... to my brother – he lives in London ....

2 My twin sister lives in Durham so she's .... on the train.

3 We try and meet up when we can especially Christmas and Easter so ...., really.

4 When we meet up we'll play tennis or squash and hockey ...., really.

5 We try and .... to meet up still.

Part C

In this recording, Lily talks about where members of her family live and how often she sees them. She also talks about her relationship with her older sister.

03

 Read the questions first, then play the recording. Are these statements true or false? Put a tick (✓) to show the correct answer.

	True	False
1 Her dad lives in the north of England.	....	✓..........
2 She has two brothers.	....	....
3 Her older sister has two children.	....	....
4 Lily does not have a good relationship with her older sister.	....	....
5 Lily and her older sister have similar personalities.	....	....

Listening tip: preparing for a true / false question

In a true / false exercise, read all the statements before you listen, and imagine how the speaker in the recording might express them.

COBUILD CHECK: 'getting on'

If you **get on** with someone, you like them and have a friendly relationship with them.

- We **get on** really well together.
- I don't **get on** with my father.
- My sister and I **get on** very well.
- Claire and I **got on** very well as children, but now we're very different.

2 Now listen again to Lily and fill in the gaps.

1 I have .... sisters.

2 My .... sister lives in the north as well.

3 We get .... really well.

4 She works at a .... quite close to her house.

5 We both .... teaching.

6 She's very interested in ....

Useful vocabulary and phrases: personality

Lily talks about her sister's personality:

'She's quite *funny*. She makes me laugh.'

'She's really *clever* and she works very hard.'

'She's quite *talkative*, like me.'

---

3 Fill in the table with a tick (✓) to show which information goes with each person.

	lives in the north of England	sees Lily once a year	makes Lily laugh	likes teaching	lives in London	lives in India
Lily						
Lily's mum						
Lily's dad						
Lily's sister						

Clear usage: 'quite'

Quite means very but not extremely. Note that Lily often uses *quite* when she is describing things:

'She works at a school *quite* close to her house.'

'She's *quite* funny. She makes me laugh.'

My review

I can understand people saying how many brothers and sisters they have.	❏
I can understand people talking about who is the youngest or oldest in their family.	❏
I can listen for details about family members, for example, where they live.	❏
I can understand people talking about relationships and personalities in their family.	❏

2 DAILY LIFE

Getting started

1 What time do you get up in the morning?
2 What things do you usually do?
3 What do you do in the evening?
4 What time do you normally go to bed?

Part A

In this recording, five people have been asked 'What time do you get up in the morning?'

04

Choose the correct answer for each person.

1 a `07:00`   b `08:00`   c `09:00`

2 a `06:00`   b `06:30`   c `06:45`

3 a `06:45`   b `07:45`   c `08:45`

4 a `09:30`   b `08:30`   c `07:30`

5 a `15:00`   b `16:00`   c `17:00`

Clear usage: 'getting up' in the morning

time	phrase	time	phrase
07:00	I get up at seven o'clock. I get up at seven a.m.	07:10	I get up at ten past seven. I get up at ten after seven. (US)
07:15	I get up at seven fifteen. I get up at quarter past seven. I get up at a quarter after seven. (US)	07:30	I get up at seven thirty. I get up at half past seven.
07:45	I get up at seven forty-five. I get up at quarter to seven. I get up at a quarter before seven. (US)	07:50	I get up at seven fifty. I get up at ten to eight. I get up at ten before eight. (US)

Part B

In this recording, Sam talks about what he usually does in the morning.

05

1 Look at the pictures, then listen to the recording. Number each picture to show Sam's daily routine.

Listening tip: using images

Photos or images can really help you to understand the context of something you are listening to.

- Look at the images before you listen and try to think of words in English that describe the things you can see.
- If you don't understand something you hear, can the image help by giving you context?
- Images can act as an equivalent to the gestures and movements you would use in a face-to-face conversation.

Clear usage: 'usually', 'normally' and 'sometimes'

If something *usually* or *normally* happens, it is the thing that most often happens.

Usually *I get up at six thirty a.m.*

*I **normally** get up at seven a.m. for work.*

Sometimes means on some occasions rather than all the time.

*I **sometimes** sit out in the garden and read.*

2 Now listen again and complete the gaps with the action words in the box. Listen carefully for the action words Sam uses, like *do*, *make*, or *have*.

have	do	check	head off	eat	jump

1 Usually the first thing I would .... is put the kettle on to make a cup of coffee.
2 Then I would .... in the shower, ... a shave.
3 Sometimes I .... breakfast.
4 And then just .... toward the train station.
5 Then I .... my email and get started for the day.

Clear usage: everyday activities

kettle = a covered container that you use for boiling water to make hot drinks, like tea or coffee.
to *put the kettle on* = to switch it on to boil water (UK)
jump in the shower = to have a quick shower
head off = to go to a place in a particular direction

Part C

In this recording, Deborah talks about her daily routine.

06

1 Read the questions first, then play the recording. Are these statements true or false? Put a tick (✓) in the correct column.

	True	False
1 Deborah travels to work by train.	✓	....
2 She normally gets to work at 7 o'clock.	....	....
3 She works in a hospital.	....	....
4 When she gets home, she cooks her dinner.	....	....
5 Then she might go to the cinema.	....	....

Clear usage: 'catching a train'

Deborah says: 'I *catch* the train'.
If you *catch* a train (or a bus or plane), you get on it in order to travel somewhere.
You may also hear *take* the train / bus, or *get* the train / bus'.
Both have the same meaning as *catch* the train / bus.

2 Listen again carefully to the recording. Match Deborah's actions to the correct times.

1 Deborah gets up at   a 16:30
2 She gets to work at   b 06:45
3 She comes home from work at c 23:00
4 She goes to bed at   d 08:30

Part D

Listen to Ana talking about her routine.

07

1 Read the questions first, then play the recording. Choose 'a' or 'b'.

1 What is Ana's job?	**a** doctor	**b** journalist
2 When does she sometimes have to work?	**a** at night	**b** at the weekend
3 She gets up at five o'clock …	**a** in the morning	**b** in the evening
4 What does Ana make after she gets up?	**a** breakfast	**b** dinner
5 She works until nine o'clock …	**a** in the morning	**b** in the evening

2 Listen again to the recording. Fill in the table with a tick (✓) to show what Ana does *before* and *after* work.

	has breakfast	watches TV	gets up	goes to bed	makes dinner	has a shower
before work						
after work						

Listening tip: stress on important words

Ana speaks quickly, but listen to how she puts more stress on the important words:

'… and I make my *dinner*, and then I watch some *TV*, and I have a *shower*, then I go to *work*.'

Ana says 'I have *a bit of* breakfast'. *A bit of* means a small amount of something. *Would you like a bit of lunch?*

My review

I can understand people talking about regular activities.	❑
I can listen for different times of day.	❑
I can understand what time of day people do things.	❑
I can understand how regularly people do things.	❑

3 CHILDHOOD

Getting started

1 What is your earliest childhood memory?
2 What activities did you enjoy?
3 How would you describe your childhood?
4 Did you do things with your parents or on your own?

Part A

In this recording, five people talk about their earliest childhood memory.

08

1 Look at the pictures of things the speakers mention. Number the pictures in the order you hear them.

2 Listen again. What expressions do they use for talking about their childhood? Find the right words / phrases in the box.

| would go   when I was   would spend   brought up   grew up   spent   would take   used to |

1 I was .... in the countryside.

2 .... five years old I learned to ride a bike and my dad, every weekend, ... me round the block on it.

3 Myself and my brother .... to the sweet shop and we .... our 50 pence.

4 The house I .... in was on the same street as the library [...] I .... spend all my time reading.

5 During my childhood I .... every weekend at the beach.

Part B

In this recording, Patrick talks about his childhood memories of growing up in North Carolina in the USA.

09

1 Tick (✓) the words Patrick uses to describe his childhood.

different .... crazy .... brilliant .... happy .... healthy ....

great .... lively .... interesting .... OK .... colourful ....

> The word *OK* (or *okay*) is used in many ways. Patrick says 'everyone was perfectly *OK with* that'. He means that the situation was acceptable to everyone.
>
> *She wanted to know if the trip was OK with the government.*

2 Read the questions first, then play the recording. Listen carefully, and take notes about Patrick's childhood. There are some pictures to help you.

pellet gun	backpack	camping gear	fishing gear

crayfish	snakes	hiking	hunting

1 Where did Patrick grow up? ....

2 What did Patrick do in the woods? ....

3 What things did Patrick own when he was ten? ....

4 What creatures did Patrick try to catch? ....

5 How old was Patrick when he could pack a backpack? ....

6 Does Patrick think his kind of childhood is a good way for children to grow up? ....

> Patrick talks about his '*fishing gear*' and '*camping gear*'.
>
> *Gear* refers to the things you need for an activity. *Fishing gear* could be a rod, a net, bait, etc. and *camping gear* could be a tent, a small stove to cook on, firelighters, etc.
>
> Other words you might hear for the same thing are *equipment* or *kit*.

3 Read the definitions below. Can you find nouns in the recording which mean the same to complete the phrase on the right?

1 The opposite of 'inside'.   ou_ _ _ _ _

2 To try and get away from someone or something.   es_ _ _ _

3 A clear difference between two things.   con_ _ _ _ _

4 Energy you put into a task.   eff_ _ _

5 The way you live your life.   life_ _ _ _ _

6 A chance to do something.   oppor_ _ _ _ _ _

A *kid* is an informal word for a child of any age. Patrick says 'if I have *kids* one day', meaning children in general. More specifically, it might be a young child who is older than a baby but younger than a teenager. Patrick says he had these adventures 'when I was a *kid*'.

Part C

In this recording, Abie talks about her childhood memories of growing up in Hong Kong.

Look at the pictures below. Listen to the recording and write the words Abie uses for each one. The first one has been done for you.

a bungalow

....

....

....

2 Read the questions first, then play the recording. Are these statements true or false? Put a tick (✓) to show the correct answer.

	True	False
1 Abie lived in a block of flats.	....	....
2 Abie's house had one floor.	....	....
3 Abie's house was in the centre of the city.	....	....
4 Abie's house was a typical Hong Kong house.	....	....
5 Abie was sometimes lonely.	....	....
6 Abie's family shopped in the markets.	....	....
7 Abie liked growing up in Hong Kong.	....	....

Clear usage: 'really'

When Abie talks about Hong Kong, she says: 'I *really* loved it,' and 'I *really* enjoyed it.' We say *really* before a verb or an adverb or an adjective to emphasize it:

*Was Hong Kong big? It was **really** big.*

*And was it expensive? Oh yes, it was **really** expensive.*

3 How does Abie describe these parts of her childhood? What describing words [adjectives] does she use?

1 The city   *big*
2 Her house   ....
3 Her garden   ....
4 The weather   ....
5 Her family   ....
6 The markets   ....
7 Her life   ....

Listening tip: adjectives

The usual position of adjectives is immediately before the noun. But many adjectives can go both before and after.

*It's a **big** city. The city is **big**.*

Putting the adjective after the noun is a way of emphasizing its importance. Abie says 'the *weather was just beautiful*'.

My review

I can understand people talking about their childhood memories. ❑
I can understand people explaining the activities they enjoyed as a child. ❑
I can follow the significance of simple descriptive words in a conversation. ❑
I can recognize the importance of some different types of emphasis in a conversation. ❑

4 LIFE CHANGES

Getting started

1 Have you had an experience which changed your life?
2 How did your life change?
3 What did you learn?
4 Was the change good or bad?

Part A

In this recording, five people answer the question 'Have you had an experience which changed your life?'

11

1 Look at the pictures. Number the pictures in the order you hear them.

Listening tip: picture questions

In a photo or picture exercise, look at all the pictures first. Ask yourself what you see in the pictures and think of the vocabulary you associate with it (a plane flying – travel, passport, journey, holiday, new country). How does the picture relate to the question? How might the people in the recording express themselves?

Part B

In this recording, Karen talks about an experience which changed her life.

12

1 Read the questions first, then play the recording. Are these statements true or false? Put a tick (✓) to show the correct answer.

		True	False
1	Karen has one child.	....	....
2	Before she was a mother work was the most important thing for Karen.	....	....
3	Karen gave up working after she became a mother.	....	....
4	Other things became important to Karen after her children were born.	....	....
5	The life change was easy for Karen.	....	....
6	Karen thinks that the life change has made her calmer and more relaxed.	....	....

Clear usage: 'before', 'when', 'still', 'as', and 'now'

Karen uses some important short words to put her story in the right order.

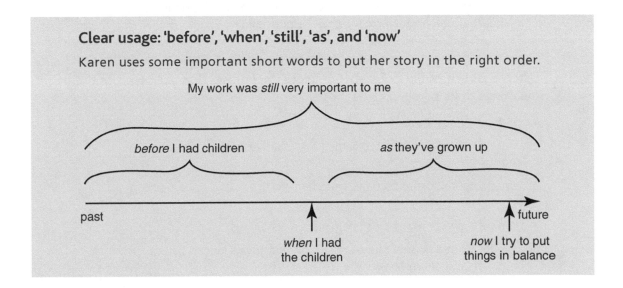

My work was *still* very important to me

before I had children   *as* they've grown up

past   future

when I had   *now* I try to put
the children   things in balance

2 Now listen again and complete the gaps in what Karen says with the words in the box. The first one has been done for you.

difficult	everything	seriously	children	important	different	priorities

1 ... before I had .... my work was .... to me.

2 When I had the children although my work was still very .... to me,

3 I think my .... changed and I started to see things in a .... way.

4 It's been .... to juggle and balance out work and home life.

5 I think now I try to put things in balance and not take things too ....

COBUILD CHECK: 'change'

- It would be unwise to make a **change** at this time.
- People, I'm asking you to please make a **change** for the better.
- In a **changing** world, we must give our workers the education and skills they need to compete.
- Sometimes we have life-**changing** choices to make.

Work–life balance means having a healthy mix of work and non-work activities in your life. Not too much or too little work, and not too much or too little relaxation. Maybe you have a similar phrase in your own language. Many employers and employees, like Karen, talk about *balancing* work and home life. And people who have a lot of home responsibilities, such as looking after children, talk about *juggling* their responsibilities.

3 Listen again carefully to Karen. Complete the phrases that she says. Use the meanings to help you.

1	all the time you have	every spare *moment*
2	making progress in your job, getting a promotion	further my c ....
3	when something else becomes important to you	my p .... changed
4	to have a different view of something	see things in a d .... w ....
5	give the right amount of time and importance to things in your life	put things in b ....
6	the opposite of 5	let things get o .... of p ....

Part C

In this recording, Abie talks about how she changed her life.

13

1 Listen for the phrases below and put them in the order you hear them.

it took up a lot of my time	......
I went back to university	......
to write books part time	......
I'm my own boss	......
I wanted to make a change	......
five or six years ago	..1..
now I write books	......

Useful vocabulary and phrases: working hours

part-time   *temporary*

full-time   *permanent*

---

2 **Listen again and answer the questions about Abie's experience.**

1 What was Abie's original job?

   a lawyer   **b** writer   **c** university teacher

2 She changed her job because …

   a it was a lot of work.   **b** it was too difficult.   **c** she had children.

3 Abie did two courses to help make a change. What were they?

   a law and writing   **b** painting and writing **c** law and painting

4 She wrote books and worked as a lawyer at the same time.

   a true   **b** false   **c** she doesn't say

5 She stopped being a lawyer to study writing at university.

   a true   **b** false   **c** she doesn't say

6 Now, Abie writes books for …

   a artists.   **b** lawyers.   **c** children.

7 Abie likes her new work because …

   a she makes more money. **b** she works less.   **c** she works in the way she likes.

Abie says 'I *found* the job a lot of hard work' and 'I *found* I enjoyed it more and more'.

By using *found* Abie means she discovered something about the experience. But she is also expressing a personal opinion, rather than a fact.

3 **Find a word in the recording which means the same as the following.**

1 Saturdays and Sundays   ……………………

2 working only some days in the week   ……………………

3 a qualification you get from university   ……………………

4 artistic   ……………………

5 with success   ……………………

My review

I can understand people talking about experiences which changed their lives.   ❏

I can understand people talking about their work-life balance.   ❏

I can listen for details about somebody's working life.   ❏

I can understand people expressing feelings about changes in their lives.   ❏

---

5 YOUR FRIENDS

Getting started

1 Who are your friends? Why are they important to you?
2 Do you have a large group of friends, or just a few 'best' friends?
3 Do you 'hang out' with your friends regularly, or do you keep in contact with them online?

Part A

In this recording, you are going to hear six people talk about their friends.

14

1 Read the questions first and then listen to the recordings one by one. What things do they mention? Tick (✓) the correct boxes.

Which speakers talk about ...	Genevieve	Fliss	Jeremy	Catherine	Laura	Chris
their friends from university?						
their friends from primary school (ages 5–11)?						
seeing their friends at the weekends?						
friends that live in other countries?						
having one 'best' friend?						
talking to their friends online?						
friends being important to them?						

> Chris says 'I try to *spend time with* my friends'. If you *spend time* with someone, you do something with them or stay with them for a period of time.

2 How do the speakers express that friends are important to them? Listen again and complete the sentences with the words and phrases in the box.

come and go	no time	lucky	catch up with	spend time with
girlfriends	keep in contact	see	lonely	communicate with

1 Genevieve: It'd be a very .... world if you didn't have someone outside of your family to ....

2 Fliss: People kind of .... in your lives but there are always certain people that stay.

3 Jeremy: It's good to have people you can relate to and ....

4 Catherine: I don't .... them very often but when we do see each other it's like .... has passed.

5 Laura: I feel very .... to have such a wonderful group of ....

6 Chris: I try to .... friends because I think it's important to ....

> Catherine says 'I don't see them [her friends] very often but when we do *see each other* it's like no time has passed'. We say *seeing each other* when we are talking about members of a group meeting or doing something together.

Clear usage: social media verbs

Chris makes verbs using the name of the internet phone service Skype, and the social network Twitter. He says 'I *skype* and *Tweet* a lot, really'. Here are some more verbs you can use to talk about using social media:

update (your status)

text (someone)

skype (someone)

post (something)

(re)tweet (something)

(un)friend (someone)

upload (a photo / video / music)

block (someone)

Part B

Eoin is from Ireland but now lives in London. In this recording, he talks about staying in touch with his friends from home.

Listen for these phrases from Section A. Number them in the order you hear them.

catch up with	....	international friends	....
spend (a lot of) time with	....	keep in contact with	....
modern technology	....	hang out	....
keep in touch	....		

2 Read the questions and answers below first. Then listen again and tick (✓) the correct answers to each question.

1 How does Eoin keep in touch with his friends in Ireland?

text ....   post ....   phone ....

2 What do they do when he visits them in Ireland?

play sports ....   go to see bands ....   go for meals ....

3 Where are his new 'international' friends from?

France ....   America ....   Poland ....

4 What social media does Eoin use to stay in touch with his friends in Ireland?

Twitter ....   Skype ....   Facebook ....

Useful vocabulary and phrases: friendship

stay in touch / contact (with)	*see*
keep in touch / contact (with)	*drop in*
catch up (with)	*drop by*
hang out (with)	*look in on*
hook up (with)	

Part C

Holly and Hannah are good friends. In this recording, they discuss friendship.

What three things do Holly and Hannah think make a good friendship? Number the ideas in the order you hear them.

giving advice and listening   ......

giving each other time on their own   ......

being honest   ......

COBUILD CHECK: 'each other'

You use **each other** to show that every member of a group does something to or for the other members.

- We looked at **each other** in silence.
- Maybe we can see **each other** later this week.
- Old friends always talk to **each other** like that.

Listening tip: listening for your turn to speak

When someone is speaking you may be listening for the right time to speak – for when it is your turn. One way that a speaker can show they have finished speaking is by making their voice go down at the end of a sentence. For example, Holly says:

'I think honesty is really important. What do *you think*?'

When a speaker pauses, that can also be a signal for you to speak. But if the speaker uses a connective word (*and ..., but ..., so ..., because ...*) or even '*um ...*' or '*uh ...*', it probably means they want to continue speaking. For example, Hannah says:

'I think that's true *because* ... I'm just thinking, there's lots of times ...'

2 How do Holly and Hannah talk about their friendship? Listen to the recordings again and complete the sentences with the words and phrases in the box.

| each other | own space | trust you | useful advice | ourselves |
| get your opinion | spend time with | close | make time | be honest |

1 Hannah: Before I leave the house […] I'll go up to your room, just to .... on what I'm wearing.

2 Hannah: That's what's really good about having such a .... friend, is because you can .... with me.

3 Holly: I go to you for advice a lot because I know I can .... and hopefully I can give you .... as well.

4 Hannah: It's sort of important we .... for each other but we also make time for ....

5 Hannah: We're very good at judging when you might want your .... and when you might want to .... friends.

6 Holly: I know it is important not to be on top of .... all the time.

My review

I can understand people describing their friends. ☐
I can recognize ways of talking about friendships. ☐
I can understand language for talking about social media. ☐
I can follow a conversation about the importance of friendship. ☐

6 YOUR HOUSE

Getting started

1 Where do you live?
2 Who do you live with?
3 What chores do you do?
4 What do you like about sharing a house?

Part A

In this recording, five people answer the question 'Who do you live with?'

Look at the pictures. Number the pictures in the order you hear them.

17   1

Clear usage: 'flat' vs 'apartment'

In the UK, a *flat* is a group of rooms where someone lives in a large building.
In the US, this is called an *apartment*.

In the UK, someone's *flatmate* is a person who shares a flat with them.
In the US, this person is called a *roommate*.

Part B

Useful vocabulary and phrases: household chores

A *chore* is a job that you have to do, especially to keep a house clean. For example:

cleaning up / (doing the) cleaning

using the washing machine

hanging the washing out

doing the dishes / doing the washing-up

hoovering

tidying up

making the bed

ironing

Now listen to Sarah talking about sharing a house.

18

1 Choose the correct answer for each of the following questions.

1 Sarah lives in ...

   a an apartment   **b** a terraced house

2 Sarah lives with ...

   a her parents   **b** two other girls

3 Living with others, the worst part is ...

   a chores   **b** communicating

4 The best part of living with others is ...

   a making new friends   **b** doing the cleaning

Sarah talks about something being 'the biggest *challenge*'.
A *challenge* is something that is difficult to do.

2 Listen again carefully to Sarah and fill in the table with a tick (✓) to show what she likes about sharing a house.

cleaning up the kitchen	making new friends	having people around	having a chat	when you just want to hang out	hanging the washing out

Clear usage: 'hang out'

There are two different meanings for the phrasal verb *hang out*, and Sarah uses it in both ways.

First, she mentions '*hanging* the washing *out*'.
This means hanging wet clothes outside to dry.

Then, Sarah also says she likes 'having people around when you just want to *hang out*'. This means to spend time with them, but not doing anything in particular. This is an informal term.

3 Now listen again and fill in the gaps in what Sarah says. Use the words in the box.

friends	cultures	chores	communication	hang

1 I find the biggest challenge in shared living would probably be the distribution of
....

2 You have different backgrounds, different ....

3 I think the best way to deal with that is ....

4 Just having people around when you just want to .... out.

5 They have friends, you have .... – it kind of brings two big circles together.

Listening tip: gap-fill exercises

- *Read* the gap-filler phrases before you listen.

- *Pause* the recording after you hear an answer.

- *Listen again* to the whole recording after you have filled in all the gaps.

4 Listen again carefully to Sarah. Match the words or phrases Sarah uses (on the left) with ones which have similar meanings (on the right).

1 shared living   a making clean

2 probably   b the feeling of being friends with someone

3 chores   c living with other people

4 cleaning up   d jobs you do in the house to keep it clean

5 generally   e in a general sense

6 friendship   f most likely

Part C

In this recording, Ana talks about sharing the chores with her husband.

1 Are these statements true or false? Put a tick (✓) to show the correct answer.

	True	False
1 Ana does the cooking.	……….	……….
2 Ana's husband does the cooking.	……….	……….
3 Ana does the washing-up.	……….	……….
4 Ana's husband does the washing-up.	……….	……….
5 Ana has only cleaned the bathroom once.	……….	……….
6 Now they don't argue about cleaning.	……….	……….

COBUILD CHECK: 'argue'

If you **argue** with someone, you disagree with them about something.

* He was **arguing** with his wife about money.
* They are **arguing** over details.
* We never **argue**.

2 Now listen again carefully to Ana. Underline the phrases that you hear.

1 I do the cooking

2 he does the cooking

3 he'd only cleaned the bathroom once

4 she never cleans up the kitchen

5 I said it wasn't acceptable

6 now we don't argue

3 Listen again to Sarah and Ana's recordings. Fill in the table below with a tick (✓) to show who mentions which chore.

	hanging out the washing	cleaning up the kitchen	doing the cooking	using the washing machine	cleaning the bathroom
Sarah					
Ana					

My review

I can understand people talking about where they live.	❏
I can understand people talking about who they live with.	❏
I can understand people talking about which chores they do.	❏
I can understand what people like about sharing a house.	❏

7 LIFE IN THE CITY

Getting started

1 What is the best thing about life in the city?
2 What is the worst thing about life in the city?
3 What is there to do in the city?
4 What would you do on your ideal day?

Part A

In this recording, Ana talks about life in her city.

1 Listen, then choose the correct answer.

1 Which city does Ana talk about?	**a** Beijing	**b** Manchester
2 How does she describe the city?	**a** small	**b** large
3 Ana says there are lots of …	**a** art exhibitions	**b** shops
4 Where Ana lives, there aren't very many …	**a** shops	**b** parks

---

Clear usage: 'lots of' and 'very little'

To show there are a large number of things, Ana says:

'There's *lots of* stuff to do.'

To show there's a small amount of something, Ana says:

'There's *very little* green space.'

---

2 Listen again and use the words in the box to fill in the blanks and complete these sentences.

many	lots	little	lots

1 There are .... of art exhibitions.
2 And .... of things on at the cinema.
3 There's very .... green space.
4 There aren't very .... parks near where I live.

Part B

In this recording, Sarah talks about the city where she lives.

1 Listen, then answer the questions to check your general understanding.

21

1 Which city does Sarah talk about?	**a** London	**b** Los Angeles
2 How does she describe the city?	**a** boring	**b** incredible
3 She dislikes …	**a** the weather	**b** the people
4 She says the people are …	**a** fantastic	**b** rude

Listening tip: people who speak quickly

Sarah speaks quickly and gives a lot of information in a short space of time. Listen to the recording several times, and each time, listen for just one piece of information.

2 Listen again to Sarah and complete the table with a tick (✓) to show which words or phrases are positive (Good) and which are negative (Bad).

	Good	Bad
incredible	………	………
not that great	………	………
awful	………	………
fantastic	………	………

Part C

Now listen to Sam talking about what he likes and dislikes about city life.

  1 Add ticks (✓) in the table below to show what Sam likes or dislikes.

22

	noise	coffee shops	restaurants	cost of life	meeting new people
likes					
dislikes					

COBUILD CHECK: 'noise'

Noise is a loud sound.

- I'll never forget the **noise** from the crowd at the end of the game.
- I can't hear you. There's too much **noise**.
- There was a lot of **noise** in the background.

2 Listen again and fill in the blanks to complete the sentences.

1 I like going to new .... and new ....

2 And it's easy to meet my .... and to meet new ....

3 One of the things I dislike most about living in town is the ....

4 And I don't like the .... in the city.

Part D

In this recording, Nikki talks about her ideal day in London.

1 Number the pictures to show the correct order of her ideal day.

Clear usage: expressing possibility

To talk about a possibility or something that may happen, Nikki says:

'I *would* go to the corner shop to buy my breakfast.'

'I *could* go to my local part of town and go to the market there.'

'I *might* go to a museum.'

Here are some more examples:

I **would** listen to music all day if I could.

I **could** go shopping for a new dress on Saturday.

I **might** call James this evening if I have time.

2 Listen again to Nikki. Are these statements true or false? Put a tick (✓) to show the correct answer.

	True	False
1 On any day, there's lots to do in the city.	....	....
2 Nikki would buy breakfast at the market.	....	....
3 You can buy clothes at the market.	....	....
4 In the afternoon, she might go to the cinema.	....	....
5 Nikki might meet friends for lunch.	....	....
6 London has some beautiful parks.	....	....

Listening tip: listening to a series of events

Nikki talks about several activities. Note how she uses *then* to introduce the next activity: '*Then* in the afternoon I might ...'; '*Then* I might go to ...'

Other words you might hear that link events are: *next*, *afterwards*, or *later*.

3 Listen again to the recording. Listen carefully to what Nikki says about the market. Fill in the table with ticks (✓) to show which things Nikki mentions that you can buy at the market.

	fresh fish	mobile phones	lunch	clothes	breakfast	kitchen-ware	furniture
Yes							
No							

Nikki says 'I could *wander* round there' and 'I might *have a wander* in one of the beautiful parks that London has'. If you *wander* in a place, you walk around there in a casual way, often without a plan.

My review

I can understand people talking about the best and worst things about life in the city. ❑

I can understand people talking about what there is to do in their city. ❑

I can understand people talking about what they would do on their ideal day. ❑

I can listen for details about what you can do or buy in a market. ❑

8 LIFE IN THE COUNTRYSIDE

Getting started

1 What does the word 'countryside' mean to you?
2 What words do you know to describe the countryside?
3 Do you live there now or have you lived there before?
4 Would you like to live there in the future?

Part A

What things remind you of the countryside? Animals? Rivers? In this recording, five people tell you what the countryside means to them.

Look at the pictures. Number the pictures in the order you hear them.

Part B

Sam comes from a place in the UK called the New Forest. What does he like about life in the countryside?

Put a tick (✓) by the things Sam mentions.

quiet	………	friendly people	………
clean air	………	hiking	………
lots to do in the evenings	………	beautiful views	………
horse-riding	………	nice food	………
going to the sea	………	trees	………

COBUILD CHECK: 'be able to'

If you **are able to** do something, you have skills or qualities that make it possible for you to do it.

- A 10-year-old should **be able to** prepare a simple meal.
- The company says they**'re able to** keep prices low.

2 Listen again to Sam. Find a word in the recording which means the same as the phrases below.

1 close to   ....

2 where the sea meets the land   ....

3 where the sea / land meets the sky ....

4 after 6 p.m.   ....

5 not in the house   ....

6 the best thing   ....

7 a break from work   ....

Clear usage: describing a place

noun + (be)	pronoun + (be)	there + (be)
the water's fresh	it's very pretty	there's plenty to see
the houses are old	they are small	there are farms

3 What words did Sam use to describe the New Forest? Fill the gaps in what he said.

1 The ....'s really clean.

2 .... beautiful views.

3 The .... friendly.

4 .... less to do in the evenings.

5 .... the ideal place to go.

Clear usage: emphasizing a feeling

Sam says: '*what I like about it* is that it's quieter and the air's really clean'. But he could just have said 'it's quieter and the air's really clean'.

Sam added *what I like about it is* to emphasize the verb *like*. He also stresses this word slightly.

***What we demand** is jobs!*

***What the people want** is peace and freedom.*

***What this place needs** is a good clean.*

Part C

In this recording, we hear Bartley. Bartley is from Teignmouth, a place by the sea in the UK. Listen to him talk about things you can find there.

1   Look at the pictures and choose the correct word for each.

| tourists | river | hotels | harbour | beach | countryside |

....

....

> Bartley says that the *fair* comes to town. The *fair* is an event that happens once a year in the town. There are goods on display at the fair which you can buy, and you can play games to win prizes. There are big, fun machines called *rides* which you can pay to use.

2   Listen again to Bartley. Are these statements true or false? Put a tick (✓) to show the correct answer.

		True	False
1	Teignmouth is a very different from other English seaside towns.	....	....
2	It has a population of 28,000.	....	....
3	Bartley thinks Teignmouth is a good place for a child.	....	....
4	Bartley thinks Teignmouth is better in winter than in summer.	....	....
5	Bartley has changed his opinion of Teignmouth now he is older.	....	....

Clear usage: describing a place with 'you have' or 'you get'

Bartley describes Teignmouth in the same way as Sam. He says: 'there's the fiesta in the harbour' and 'it's very pretty'.

But he also uses an informal way of describing a place. He says: *'you have* the beach, *you have* a river, *you have* the countryside' and *'you get* people that come on holiday'.

You have and *you get* is the same as saying *you can see (the following things:).* This is common in spoken English, but not in written English.

27

3 Bartley now compares Teignmouth to London. He talks about the things he 'misses' – the things he is sad he does not have now. Listen and write down the things Bartley misses.

....

4 Listen again. First, find the missing word in the expression on the left. Then match them with the meanings on the right.

1 you really *miss*
2 I took it for ....
3 you ....
   that every day
4 but it makes you ....
   .... more

a did not see how valuable and good it was
b see something unusual
c realize how valuable and good something was
d feel sad because you do not have something you used to have

Useful vocabulary and phrases: things you miss from the past

It's sad that the area is not as quiet as it used to be.

I'm sorry that I don't live next to a river any more.

Thinking about it now, I had a wonderful childhood.

I regret not staying in touch with old friends.

Looking back, the city used to be much dirtier than it is now.

I took it for granted that I could visit them easily.

My review

I can recognize common vocabulary for talking about the countryside. ❑

I can understand language describing what a person likes about a place. ❑

I can recognize language used to talk about somewhere you miss. ❑

9 LIVING IN ANOTHER COUNTRY

Getting started

1 Have you ever lived in another country?
2 If you have, what was different about that country?
3 What new experiences did you have?
4 Did the experience change you?

Part A

In this recording, five people speak about a part of their life they spent living in another country.

28

Which country or city did they live in and how long did they live there for?

	Country or city?	How long?
1	Japan	1 year
2		
3		
4		
5		

Listening tip: listening for numbers

If you are listening for key information like numbers, ask yourself what the number might be: small numbers or big numbers. Will they be spoken as cardinal numbers (*one*, *two*, *three*, etc.) or ordinal numbers (*first*, *second*, *third*, etc.)? Think about the words which they might say with the number (e.g. *years old*, *hours*, *people*, *per cent*) and listen for them in the audio.

Part B

In this recording, Pauline, from New Zealand, speaks about how she went to live in Austria when she was a student.

29

Read the questions and listen for the numbers in her story.

1 How old was Pauline when she went to Austria? ....
2 How many hours was the flight from New Zealand to Austria? ....
3 How many years did she live with the family in Austria? ....
4 How old were the little boy and little girl in the Austrian family? .... and ....
5 How many people lived in the small Austrian village? ....

Pauline says she had a *host* brother and sister. A *host* family is a family who invite someone, often a student from another country, to stay with them in their home.

Useful vocabulary and phrases: away from home

I'm *homesick*.
I want to give (someone) a call.

I have *jetlag*.
I got up at 3 in the morning and I'm tired.

I love *backpacking*.
I'm an *independent traveller*.

I'm staying with a *host family* in the town.
I'm at the *hostel* in the centre of the city.

---

2 Listen again to Pauline and read the statements below. Are these statements true or false? Put a tick (✓) to show the correct answer.

		True	False
1	Pauline had a job in Austria.	....	....
2	Pauline couldn't speak German well before she got to Austria.	....	....
3	Pauline knew a lot about Austria before she went there.	....	....
4	Pauline lived in somebody's house in Austria.	....	....
5	Pauline was often unhappy in Austria.	....	....

Clear usage: 'used to'

Pauline says: 'it was very different to what I was *used to*'.

In unit 3 you heard 'I *used to* spend all my time reading'. They are using *used to* in two different ways.

Pauline says *used to* to talk about a situation she is familiar with, that she knows very well. *Used to* + noun.

*I have lived here in this city for two years, so I'm **used to** the noise and traffic.*

In unit 3 the speaker says *used to* to talk about something she often did in the past, but does not do now. *Used to* + verb.

*When I was young I **used to** wear short trousers.*

3 Listen again. Think about the true and false answers in exercise 2. Look at the pictures and complete the sentences.

Action	Sentence
	I went to .... there.
	I learned to speak another ....
	I got to know another ....
	I lived with a ....
	I didn't get very ....

Part C

On the next two tracks, Celia speaks about how she left England to live in Japan for a 'gap year'.

1 Read the questions and choose the best ending to each sentence.

1 During a gap year, students often ...   **a** study.   **b** go travelling.
2 In Japan, Celia lived ...   **a** with her friends.   **b** with a Japanese family.
3 Celia worked in Japan ...   **a** at a school.   **b** at a company.
4 Celia stayed in Japan ...   **a** for a year.   **b** for eighteen years.
5 Celia thought that Japanese and English family life ...   **a** were similar.   **b** were different.

2 The sentences below gave you the answers to exercise 1. Listen again and complete the missing phrase.

1 They often work to save enough money and then sometimes they ....
2 I stayed with a Japanese family who were .... of ....
3 Once I was out there I was able to earn money ....
4 I was away for a ....
5 I was living with a Japanese family who were .... from my family.

COBUILD CHECK: 'gap'

A **gap** is a space between two things:

- There was a narrow **gap** between the curtains.
- His horse escaped through a **gap** in the fence.

A **gap year** is a period of time during which a student takes a break from studying after they have finished school and before they start college or university. This expression is mainly British.

- I went around the world in my **gap year**.

  31

3 Read the summary of track 31 below and think about what words might be missing. Listen to the recording and find the words to fill the gaps in this summary.

Celia's time in Japan made her think about Japanese and English ....
and also about who she was – her .... She began to
.... her own English family more. Her Japanese host parents were very
.... and didn't allow their children much ....
or ....

Listening tip: false starts

You have heard *ums* and *uhs* in the recordings and also repeated words (see transcript for how these appear in the recording). Another feature of natural speech is *false starts*. This is when a speaker might begin a sentence, and then change the way they express themselves in the middle.

They may change a word. Celia changes *when* for *once*: 'And then *when – once* I was out there I was able to ...'

They may add a phrase. Celia adds *for me*: 'Um ... it ... *for me* it was ... um ... the first time I'd been away from my family.'

Or they may stop completely and restart the sentence. Celia says: 'It just gave me a real ... um ... It allowed me to look in depth in – into Japanese culture.'

My review

I can understand someone talking about living in another country.	❏
I can listen for numbers in someone's speech.	❏
I can identify phrases and ideas about travelling.	❏
I can understand someone expressing how they feel about living abroad.	❏

10 GETTING AROUND

Getting started

1 Can you ask how to get somewhere?
2 Would you understand the answer?
3 Can you name landmarks and buildings often found in cities?
4 Can you understand directions on the phone?

Part A

In this recording, you will hear Shawn, a visitor to London from the United States, asking directions to different places.

32

Look at the pictures. Listen to the recording and write the name of the location under the picture.

....

....

Clear usage: imperative sentences

When listening to directions you will often hear the sentence start with a verb. This is the most common way of giving clear instructions.

go up this road here   *keep on* going down

walk for about five minutes   *take the* first left

American English and British English sometimes use different words for the same thing – here the American speaker says 'Where is the closest *movie theatre* here?' The other (British) person replies 'Oh, you mean the *cinema*?'

  2 Look at the signs and directions below. Listen to the recording and write the number next to the correct picture.

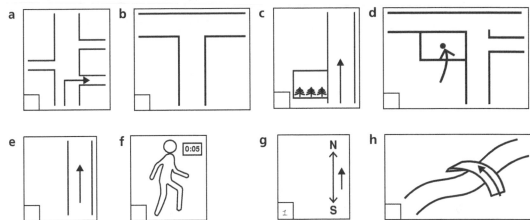

a   b   c   d

e   f   g   h

  3 Look at the map below and listen to the full recording of Shawn asking for directions. Number the places on the map for each of the directions that are given.

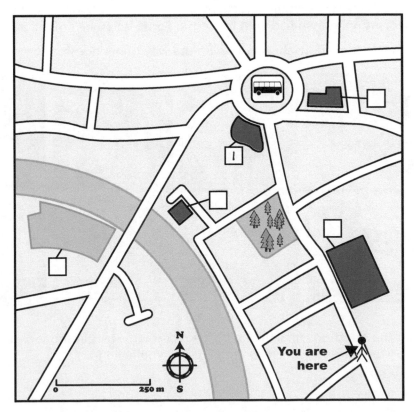

4 What else did you remember? Fill in the missing information from these sentences. Listen again to the recording if you can't remember.

1 The Apollo Theatre is about .... hundred metres away.

2 The cinema is called .... Studios.

3 The hospital is a big .... building.

4 The hotel is on a road called ....

5 You can get to the sports ground by ....

Part B

Now let's try some longer directions given over the phone. Listen to the phone conversation Shawn had with his cousin Lorna when he arrived at the airport.

35

1 Tick (✓) the locations she mention on the way to her house.

2 Read the questions first, then play the recording. The questions check your general understanding. Play the recording again if you need to.

1 Where is Shawn?

   a At the airport.   **b** At Lorna's house.   **c** In America.

2 Where is Shawn going?

    a To the airport.   **b** To Lorna's house   **c** Piccadilly

3 Where does Lorna live?

    a Heathrow   **b** Piccadilly   **c** Hammersmith

4 Which type of transport does Shawn take?

    a Tube   **b** Bus   **c** Taxi

5 What luggage does Shawn have?

    a one suitcase   **b** one backpack   **c** two backpacks

6 What road does Lorna live on?

    a Fulham Palace Road   **b** Charing Cross Road   **c** Ellaline Road

7 What colour is Lorna's door?

    a Red   **b** Blue   **c** Black

Clear usage: 'if' sentences

When giving directions many people use some *if*-sentences (conditionals) instead of the imperative.

Adding a few of these sounds a little more polite. Lorna says:

'*if* you head for the tube stop, you'll see signs for the underground'.

'*if* you pass the supermarket, […] that'll take you out the right exit of the shopping centre'.

3 Complete Shawn's notes of the way to Lorna's house.

Take the .... line from the airport. Get off at
.... station.
Take the exit marked for the .... , go through the
....
Walk down Fulham Palace Road for .... minutes.
Past the park on your .... , and a hospital on your
....
Take the .... turn on the right after the
....
Lorna's house – .... from the end on the left.

My review

I can recognize the name of places and landmarks around the city. ❏

I can understand simple directions. ❏

I can follow a series of directions. ❏

11 STUDYING AND LEARNING

Getting started

1 What/where have you studied previously?
2 What have you learned to do – e.g. play a musical instrument or drive a car?
3 What should someone do if they want to learn this?

Part A

In this recording, five people answer the question 'What have you studied previously?' or 'Where have you studied previously?'

36

1 Look at the words below. Number the photos in the order you hear them.

English

Music

University of Exeter

Argentina

English & Biology

2 Listen again carefully to the five people. Match the subject or location (on the left) with the correct phrase (on the right).

1	English	a	'the university in Buenos Aires'
2	English and Biology	b	'I studied music'
3	Argentina	c	'I did two degrees there'
4	University of Exeter	d	'a double major'
5	Music	e	'I really enjoyed it'

One of the speakers mentions *a double major*. At a university or college in the United States, a student's *major* is the main subject that they are studying. A *double major* means that two main subjects are being studied.

Part B

Kerry is from New York. She recently completed an MBA at university.

37

 Listen to the recording. Choose the correct answer for each of the following questions.

1	MBA stands for	**a** Masters of Business Administration	**b**	Marine Biology Association
2	Kerry studied at	**a** the University of Cambridge	**b**	the University of Oxford
3	You can do an MBA	**a** anywhere in Europe	**b**	anywhere in the world
4	Kerry studied for	**a** two years	**b**	twelve months
5	The work is	**a** stressful	**b**	easy

Listening tip: multiple-choice answers

Look at all the possible answers and imagine how they might sound. *Listen* carefully before you decide which answer you hear. *Listen again* to check your answers.

 COBUILD CHECK: 'attend'

If you **attend** a school, college, or university, you go there regularly.

- They **attended** college together.
- Their children **attend** private schools.
- She moved east to **attend** university.

2 Now listen again and fill in the gaps in what Kerry says. Use the words in the box below.

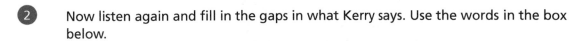

working	doing	did	attended	learn	offer

1 When I was .... my MBA.

2 I .... full time for about one year at the university.

3 Most universities .... the MBA as a two-year course.

4 although the one I .... was twelve months.

5 It is also, for some, sort of a break from work and a chance to .... something new.

6 And oftentimes the friendships you form when .... so hard can be the most rewarding part.

> Kerry uses the word *oftentimes*. This is an American word. It has the same meaning as *often*.

3 Complete the table to give the correct details about what Kerry did.

Name:	
University:	
Course of study:	
Number of months:	

Clear usage: 'study' vs 'learn'

	study	learn
meaning	spend time learning about a particular subject	get knowledge or a skill
common patterns	'study' + (subject)	'learn' + 'about' + (subject) 'learn' + 'to' + (verb)
examples	She **studied** History and Economics. He **is studying** Music at university.	She **learned about** History and Economics. I **learned to** drive a car when I was seventeen.

Part C

Useful vocabulary and phrases: learning to play a musical instrument

chord (= musical notes played at the same time)

lesson (= a time when you learn something)

play along (= produce music while listening to music)

cover (= to play or record a new version of an old song)

Dave is from Northern Ireland. In the recording, he offers advice to anyone wanting to learn to play the guitar.

 1 Listen to the recording. Are these statements true or false? Put a tick (✓) to show the correct answer.

		True	False
1	Dave has been playing the guitar for ten years.	....	....
2	He recommends that you don't learn chords.	....	....
3	You should play along with music you like.	....	....
4	He recommends lessons.	....	....
5	He recommends playing music with friends.	....	....
6	You should learn just two or three chords.	....	....

2 Match each phrase on the left with one on the right to create a list of the advice that Dave gives.

1 Take some time to ...   a lessons.
2 I wouldn't really recommend ...   b friends playing different instruments.
3 Try to play along with ...   c learn chord structures.
4 Get together with your ...   d what you like.

> Dave says 'you could even *get together* with some of your friends'. This means you could meet with friends.

3 Now listen again and fill in the gaps in what Dave says. Use the words in the box below.

trying	playing	taking	learn	get together

1 I've been .... the guitar for about ten years now.
2 I would recommend just .... some time to learn the chord structures.
3 and then .... to learn some of the chords to the music that you like.
4 It's more fun initially to just .... the basics and try to play along with what you like.
5 You could even .... with some of your friends playing different instruments.

Clear usage: 'should' + (verb)

Dave says: 'You *should* learn probably about six or seven chords'. You use *should* when you are describing *the best thing to do* in a particular situation.

You **should** exercise more.   We **should** wait a while longer.
You **shouldn't** stay up so late.   What **should** I do?

My review

I can understand people talking about what they studied.   ❏
I can understand people talking about where they studied.   ❏
I can understand people talking about something they learned.   ❏
I can understand people giving advice about learning something new.   ❏

12 STARTING WORK

Getting started

1 What was your first job? Did you like it?
2 What questions might employers ask you?
3 What skills or qualities do employers look for?
4 What's it like to look for a job? Is it difficult or easy?

Part A

In this recording, you will hear the speaker ask five questions about your first job.

39

1 The following answers were given to these questions. Write the number of the question they answer.

- I was sixteen years old. ....
- About 8 weeks. ....
- I hated the whole job. ....

- I worked in a toy store. ....
- About $5.50 an hour. ....

40

2 Look at the table below. Listen to five speakers answer the questions and complete the table.

Where was your first job?	How old were you?	How much were you paid?	How long did you spend there?	Did you enjoy it?
smoked salmon factory	16	£3.50	1 day	No
.... store	✕			
.... kiosk		✕	✕	

Where was your first job?	How old were you?	How much were you paid?	How long did you spend there?	Did you enjoy it?
.... restaurant				
expensive				

Part B

Rosie works in Human Resources. When people want to work for her company, she asks them certain questions.

41

1 Listen to the questions Rosie asks. Number each question in the order you hear them.

What qualifications do you have? ....

Do you have a valid driving licence? ....

What experience do you have that is relevant for this role? ....

And can you tell me what you know about the company already? ....

Have you worked in a similar job before? ....

Are you able to work in the evenings or the weekends? ....

2 Listen again carefully to Rosie's questions. Match the words she uses (on the left) with words or phrases with similar meanings (on the right).

1	experience	**a**	important
2	qualifications	**b**	acceptable
3	relevant	**c**	card that shows you are allowed to drive
4	company	**d**	knowledge or skill in a job you have done for a long time
5	valid	**e**	exam results or skills
6	driving licence	**f**	business

Part C

Now listen to Caroline, who is a manager in a large business based in London. She is currently looking for someone to work for her company.

1 Caroline talks about the most important things she is looking for. Put a tick (✓) next to the things Caroline mentions.

communication skills ....   experience   ....
technical skills   ....   driving licence   ....
research   ....   qualifications   ....
dressing smartly   ....   handshake   ....

Clear usage: present continuous + 'at the moment'

Caroline says: 'I'm recruiting *at the moment*'. This means she is looking *now* for someone to work for her company. Note that she uses the present continuous form (*recruiting*) to show that this is something she is doing now.

---

2 Listen again carefully to Caroline. Circle the correct word to complete each phrase that she uses.

1 It's a *junior / senior / part-time* position, within a sales team.

2 I'm looking for somebody who is a good *writer / speaker / communicator*.

3 Somebody who gets on with people, and also is willing to *learn / work / study*.

4 Somebody who's thought about the company that they're going to work for, so they've done some *thinking / research / work*.

5 *Age / Experience / Personality* is important when you're employing somebody.

6 It's important to think about how *you look / you behave / you're dressed*.

7 Dressing *smartly / casually / formally* gives a good impression.

8 A handshake is very important 'cause it gives a *bad / positive / negative* impression.

Part D

In this recording, Sara talks about looking for a job.

1 Read the statements first, and then play the recording. Are these statements true or false? Put a tick (✓) to show the correct answer.

	True	False
1 Sara has a job now.	....	....
2 Sara has worked for a long time.	....	....
3 Sara thinks it is easy to find a job.	....	....
4 Sara is hopeful she will get a job.	....	....
5 Sara works for charities.	....	....

Sara says she has 'an updated *CV*'. A *CV* is the sheet of information that shows an employer all about your education, work experience and qualifications. In America and some other English-speaking countries, it is called a *résumé*.

2 What information does Sara give? Read the questions below. You can tick (✓) more than one answer.

1 Where does Sara look to find a job?

agencies ....   websites ....   on TV ....

2 What advantages does Sara have?

friends with jobs ....   good qualifications ....   lots of experience ....

3 What advice does Sara give?

have an updated CV ....   call employers ....   be disciplined ....

4 What does Sara say makes it hard to find a job?

bad employers ....   a lot of unemployment ....   not being organized ....

Clear usage: 'have to' + (verb)

Sara says: 'you *have to be* very disciplined with yourself – you *have to make sure* that you don't just sleep in'.

You use *have to* + (the infinitive of the verb) when you want to say that it is very important that something is done. For example:

*I **have to get** to work before eight. My boss is very strict.*

*You'll **have to study** hard if you want to pass your exams.*

3 Listen again. What verbs does Sara use to talk about trying to find a job? Find the right words / phrases in the box.

comes up	have to	make sure	have to	applying for	looking for	look for

1 I don't need to .... very long in order to get a job.

2 I .... seven years of work experience.

3 If a job .... in that sector I have a good chance of getting it.

4 depending on which job I'm ....

5 .... a job can be quite hard.

6 So you .... be very disciplined.

7 .... that you're applying every single day.

My review

I can understand people talking about their first jobs.   ❏

I can understand questions an employer might ask.   ❏

I can understand language about important skills or qualities that employers look for.   ❏

I can understand people talking about looking for a job.   ❏

13 WORKING FROM HOME

Getting started

1 Do you work from home?
2 If you don't, would you like to and why?
3 Is there anything you wouldn't like about it?

Part A

In this recording, you will hear four people talk about working from home.

44

1 Number the photos in the order you hear them.

Furniture maker   **Translator**   **Caterer**   **Childminder**

2 Listen again. Use the speaker's words to answer the questions below.

1 What does the first speaker help the kids do? ....

2 What does the second speaker translate into German? ....

3 What does the third speaker prepare for her clients? .... and ....

4 What types of furniture does the fourth speaker make? ...., ...
and ....

Part B

In this recording, Abie talks about working from home as a writer.

45

1 Look at the table below and fill in the information about her work.

How long?	Why?	Job
Good points	**Bad points**	**Does she enjoy it?**

COBUILD CHECK: 'suits'

If something **suits you**, it is the best thing for you in a particular situation.

- I love my country. I like it there. It **suits me**.
- It was an arrangement which **suited them** both.

② Listen again and complete the phrases using the definitions on the right.

1	a long	the journey to work
2	I'm .... there	organized and ready
3	.... at your desk	unable to move
4	.... the children after school	collect
5	.... the work	going very fast
6	I'm quite .... at home	doing a lot of work

③ Abie uses the words and phrases in the box to give reasons and explain things. Use them to complete what she says. You might have to use them more than once.

means	because	just to	in that	'cause	so

1 ... it suits me very well .... I've small children, ... I have to take them to school.

2 ... working from home .... I'm nearer to their school.

3 I'm a writer .... it's quite easy for me to work from home.

4 ... go to the shop and buy something small .... get out of the house.

5 .... you feel a bit stuck at your desk otherwise.

6 But often the day goes very quickly .... I'm racing through the work.

7 You have to be quite self-disciplined .... you're the one that makes yourself ...

Useful vocabulary and phrases: giving reasons and explanations

Because, since and *as* are normally followed by a verb:

I make furniture *because* I *enjoy* it.

Childminding suits me *since* I really *love* kids.

I'm going back to work *as* I *need* the money.

Because of, due to and *thanks to* are normally followed by a noun:

Because of *the weather*, the event was cancelled.

I can't finish the job on time *due to circumstances* beyond my control.

The book sold well *thanks to an excellent translation*.

Part C

Dave also works at home. Does he have a similar experience to Abie?

46

Are these statements true for Abie and Dave? Tick (✓) the boxes which you think are true.

	Abie	Dave
They work from home every day.		
It's a long way from their homes to work / the city.		
They use a computer for work.		
They stay in touch with work during the day.		
They like to see people during the day.		
They prefer to work at home all the time.		

2 Complete the gaps in what Dave says with the verbs in the box.

access	rely on	provides	keep up with	connect into	do

1 My company .... remote access.

2 I .... the network ...

3 ... and .... all the same files.

4 It was pretty easy to .... things.

5 Go out and .... errands.

6 You kind of .... email.

Clear usage: 'kind of'

Dave says: 'you *kind of* rely on email'. *Kind of* is an informal expression meaning the same as 'a little' or 'in some way'. You will hear it a lot in spoken English, but not often in written English. You may hear it:

before adjectives: *It's **kind of** dark in here. Turn on the light.*

before verbs: *I **kind of** need my book for my homework. Can I have it back?*

before adverbs: *He left the shop **kind of** quickly when he saw the police officer coming in.*

---

3 Like Abie, Dave also gives reasons and explanations using *because* and *so*. Listen again and note down what Dave is explaining.

1 I work from home because ....

2 It's about an hour's drive so ....

3 It's good 'cause ....

4 I do miss being able to just go up to someone and ask a question, because ....
....

5 It can be hard to stay motivated, just because .... so
....

Clear usage: 'because' and 'so'

We use *because* to introduce a reason for a situation:

[result] *because* [reason]

*I work from home **because** I live quite far from my office.*

*It's quite easy for me to work from home **because** I'm a writer.*

We use *so* to introduce the result of a reason:

[reason] *so* [result]

*I live quite far from my office **so** I sometimes work from home.*

*I'm a writer **so** it's quite easy for me to work from home.*

---

4 What does Dave think will happen in the future? Read the statements first, then play the recording. Are these statements true or false? Put a tick (✓) to show the correct answer.

		True	False
1	Dave thinks that in the future more people will work from home.	....	....
2	Dave thinks people don't work well when they are at home.	....	....
3	Dave thinks working from home makes people happy.	....	....
4	When Dave is in the office he always talks to people before sending them an email.	....	....

Dave says that 'you can *access* everything you need to' from home. This means that you have everything you need to do your job from home. If you *access* information on a computer, you find or get it.

My review

I can listen for basic details when someone describes their job. ❏

I can identify particular vocabulary about homeworking. ❏

I can compare descriptions of people's experiences of work. ❏

I can understand when someone is giving reasons or explanations. ❏

---

14 YOUR CAREER

Getting started

1 What job do you do?
2 What did you do before that?
3 How did you find it?
4 What would you like to do in the future?

Part A

In this recording, Hazel talks about her job.

Answer the questions to test your general understanding.

1 Hazel works for
    a a bank
    b a supermarket

2 She works in
    a the finance department
    b the sales department

3 She has worked there for
    a three years
    b four years

4 Her days are
    a quite long
    b quite short

5 She looks after a team of
    a six people
    b three people

6 She finds her job
    a demanding
    b relaxing

Clear usage: 'for' and 'in'

- Hazel works *for* a supermarket (= she is employed by the company)
- Hazel works *in* the finance department (= this is the place where she works)
- Hazel works *in* finance (= her job is related to this industry)

2 Listen again carefully to Hazel. She talks about the past, present and future. Fill in the gaps using the correct word from the box.

help	like	continue	wanted	would	decided	worked

1 So I've .... there for four years.

2 I .... to work there because I .... to work in finance.

3 There's quite a lot of stuff that I have to kind of .... them with.

4 I quite .... it and it's busy all the time, so that's good.

5 So, at some point in the future I .... like to have children.

6 I think I will .... to do my job.

3 Listen again to the recording. Hazel uses several expressions relating to time. Which of the following expressions does she use?

1	in the past	....	**5**	a lot of hours	....
2	in the future	....	**6**	a few hours	....
3	for four years	....	**7**	all the time	....
4	for many years	....	**8**	at the moment	....

Part B

Now listen to Patrick talking about his previous job working with customers.

49

1 Which of these statements best describes how Patrick feels?

a Working with customers was always very pleasant.

b Working with customers was sometimes pleasant and sometimes stressful.

c Working with customers was always very stressful.

Useful vocabulary and phrases: describing jobs

Positive	Negative
demanding	*difficult*
challenging	*dull*
busy	*slow*
pleasant	*stressful*

---

2 Listen again to both Hazel and Patrick. They use positive and negative adjectives to describe their jobs. Complete the table with a tick (✓) to show who uses each adjective.

	demanding	pleasant	busy	stressful	challenging
Hazel					
Patrick					

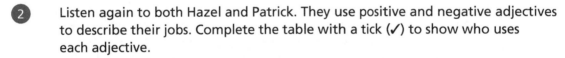

COBUILD CHECK: 'deal with'

When you **deal with** something or someone, you give your attention to them.

• Could you **deal with** this customer, please?

• We make sure that any complaints are **dealt with** quickly and fairly.

• I'm not sure I can **deal with** that right now.

• We need to take care when **dealing with** financial matters.

• How are you going to **deal with** this situation?

3   Listen again carefully to Patrick. He talks about how he dealt with customers. Fill in the gaps using the correct word/phrase from the box.

happy	complain	face to face	deal with	stressful	requested

1   I had to deal with customers .... on a daily basis.

2   Dealing with customers could be quite ....

3   A lot of my job as a manager was to .... their complaints.

4   I didn't have the pleasure of dealing with the people who were .... all the time.

5   ... but just the people who .... to speak with the manager.

6   So that they could .... about whatever issue was troubling them.

Part C

Mary works for a university. In this recording, Mary talks about retirement. Listen to the recording.

50

Are these statements true or false? Put a tick (✓) to show the correct answer.

	True	False
1 Mary could stop working soon.	....	....
2 She is not entitled to a pension.	....	....
3 Universities are hiring more staff.	....	....
4 Mary likes the idea of retirement.	....	....

> Mary says 'I'm not far off *retirement* now'. *Retirement* is when people leave their job and usually stop working completely. In the UK, the standard age for retirement is around 65. What about where you're from?

Listening tip: matching words with similar meanings

When you are matching words or phrases, here are some tips to help you find the correct answer:

- *Read* all the words and phrases before you listen.

- *Listen* carefully to how the words or phrases are used to help you understand their meanings.

Once you have matched these words and you know what they mean, try to use them yourself in a sentence.

2   Listen carefully to Mary again. Match the words or phrases Mary uses (on the left) with ones which have similar meanings (on the right).

1	not far off	**a**	allowed
2	retirement	**b**	reducing the number of
3	pension	**c**	fast and busy
4	entitled	**d**	activities you enjoy
5	cutting down on	**e**	money you receive after you stop working
6	hurried	**f**	(an action) done because someone else has made you do it
7	do things you want	**g**	close to
8	forced	**h**	the time when you stop working

Mary says that she *doesn't mind* if she has to retire.

If you *don't mind* something, you don't feel annoyed or angry about it. You feel relaxed about it.

Other examples:

• *It was hard work, but she didn't mind.*

• *I don't mind the hot weather.*

3   Listen again carefully to Mary. Choose the correct word to complete each phrase that Mary uses.

1   I'm not far off *retirement / pension / university* now.

2   I could take a *retirement / pension / holiday* now. I'm entitled to one.

3   There may not even be any *food / money / work* come September.

4   Universities are cutting down on the *staff / workers / employees*.

5   It *will / could / might* be a forced retirement!

6   ... but I don't *mind / care / know* really.

7   It'll be nice just to have a less hurried *job / day / life*.

8   ... a little bit more of the things you *want / need / like*.

My review

I can understand people talking about where they work and what they do.   ❑

I can understand people talking about previous jobs.   ❑

I can understand how people feel about their jobs.   ❑

I can understand people talking about what they will do in the future.   ❑

15 YOUR FUTURE

Getting started

1 If you could live anywhere, where would you choose?
2 If you could do anything, what would you do?
3 What would be your ideal job?
4 Why would you like to do these things?

Part A

Oscar is from Sweden. He lives in London now. In this recording, he talks about where he would like to live and what he would like to do in the future.

 51 ①

Listen to the recording then answer the questions to test your general understanding.

1 Oscar currently works with ...

  a animals   **b** computers   **c** children

2 He would like to live ...

  a in the city   **b** in the countryside   **c** near the ocean

3 He says that in London, there's not a lot of ...

  a people   **b** nature   **c** money

4 He'd like to work as ...

  a a doctor   **b** a teacher   **c** a blacksmith

5 He'd like to create things with ...

  a his hands   **b** machines   **c** other people

6 He'd feel better because of ...

  a the money he'd get   **b** the exercise he'd get   **c** the people

Oscar talks about the job of a *'blacksmith'*. A *blacksmith* is a person whose job is making things out of metal.

2 Listen again carefully to Oscar. Match the words he uses (on the left) with the correct meanings (on the right).

1	IT professional	**a**	things that you hold in your hands and use to do a particular kind of work
2	nature	**b**	very attractive to look at
3	tools	**c**	a person who works with computers
4	physical	**d**	a feeling that you have made or done something special
5	a sense of accomplishment	**e**	trees, plants, and animals
6	beautiful	**f**	connected with a person's body, not their mind

Listening tip: matching words to meanings

- *Listen* carefully for each word or phrase as it is spoken in the recording.
- Try to *listen* to the whole sentence to help you understand the meaning of the word or phrase.
- *Listen* to the whole recording – the word or phrase may be repeated.

Clear usage: conditional form

Oscar uses the conditional form: 'It *would be* very physical'.

We use the conditional form of verbs to talk about situations that do not exist now, but may exist in the future:

'would' + (**verb**), e.g. *I would feel* happy

'would like to' + (**verb**), e.g. *I would like to go* there.

3 Listen again to Oscar. Decide if each of these words and statements are about his current job or his ideal job. Put a tick (✓) in the correct column.

		current job	ideal job
1	blacksmith	....	....
2	IT professional	....	....
3	in the countryside	....	....
4	works with hands	....	....
5	makes tools from metal	....	....
6	can't create anything you can touch	....	....
7	can create something beautiful	....	....
8	in the city	....	....
9	fixes computers	....	....

COBUILD CHECK: 'ideally'

If you say that **ideally** something should happen, you mean that you would like it to happen, but know it may not be possible.

- **Ideally**, I'd like the bathroom to be even bigger.
- People should, **ideally**, eat much less fat.

 Listen again carefully to Oscar. What verbs does Oscar use to talk about what he would like to do? Find the right verbs in the box.

feel	like	be	be	move	work

1 Ideally I would like to .... away from London, where I live now.

2 What I would .... about living in the countryside is probably the clean air.

3 I would like to .... as a blacksmith.

4 It would .... very nice to work as a blacksmith.

5 I would probably .... exhausted at the end of the day.

6 I think I would .... much better if I were a blacksmith.

Part B

Laura is from Los Angeles in America. She talks about her ideal job and why she would like to do this.

  Are these statements true or false? Put a tick (✓) to show the correct answer.

		True	False
1	Laura currently works in real estate in Los Angeles.	....	....
2	She currently works as a travel blogger.	....	....
3	She would like to work as a professional travel blogger.	....	....
4	She enjoys sharing her photos and experiences with other people.	....	....
5	She would like to work as a doctor.	....	....
6	She went to the Croatian Islands last summer.	....	....
7	She is planning a trip to the Croatian Islands next summer.	....	....

Laura talks about *travel blogging*. *Blogging* is the activity of writing a *blog*. A *blog* is a website that describes the daily life of the person who writes it, and also their thoughts and ideas. A *travel blogger* is someone who writes a blog about travel.

2 Listen again carefully to Laura. Choose the correct word to complete each phrase that she uses.

1 If I could pick anything to do, I'd love to get paid to *write / travel / talk*.

2 I would love to create my own website and be able to *share / view / create* and upload photos.

3 When you're on travel *advice / writing / blogging* sites you're hearing from so many different people.

4 "Wow, you know what? If she liked it, I know I'm gonna *love / like / hate* it."

5 You know, next summer I'm already planning a trip with my girlfriends to the Croatian *capital / Islands / coast*.

6 When I get back from there I just can't wait to *post / send / print* all the photos about the places I've been.

7 There are so many things, um, I would love to *speak / write / talk* about.

8 If I could get paid to do that, I can't think of a *good / better / worse* job on the planet.

> Laura says she 'just *can't wait*'. If you *can't wait* to do something, you are very excited about it.

3 Listen again carefully to Laura. Match the words she uses (on the left) with the correct meanings (on the right).

1	to get paid	a	feel that you understand someone
2	professional	b	be given money for doing something
3	get caught up in	c	a permanent job
4	hype	d	become influenced by
5	relate to one person	e	publicity or advertising to make people interested
6	post	f	send information to a website

4 Listen again to Laura. Complete the table with ticks (✓) to show which information about her trip Laura thinks she might share.

videos	the wildlife	the nightlife	the beaches	places she's been	places she ate in	places she swam	photos

---

My review

I can understand people talking about where they would like to live in the future. ❑

I can understand people talking about what work they would like to do in the future. ❑

I can understand people describing their ideal job. ❑

I can understand people's reasons for wanting to do particular things. ❑

---

16 FOOD

Getting started

1 What's your favourite food?
2 Do you enjoy cooking?
3 What words do you know for describing food?
4 Do you prefer the food of another culture?

Part A

In this recording, you will hear people talking about their favourite type of food or meal.

Put the name of the type of food or meal under the correct picture. You can listen as many times as you like.

53

....

Part B

In this recording, Abie talks about making pancakes for her children at the weekend.

What ingredients does Abie mention? Tick (✓) the photos.

54

☐   ☐   ☐   ☐   ☐

☐   ☐   ☐   ☐   ☐

COBUILD CHECK: 'reminds me'

If something **reminds you** of another person or event, it has features which make you think of them or it.

- It's the first record I ever had and it **reminds me** of my childhood.
- He **reminds me** of myself.
- It **reminds me** of the movie 'Jaws' where the mayor didn't want to tell the tourists that there was a shark in the water.

2 Listen again. What measurements does Abie use?

1 .... of plain flour

2 .... or so of baking power

3 .... of sugar

4 .... eggs

5 .... of butter

6 .... of milk

Useful vocabulary and phrases: food measurements

Some food measurements in recipes are related to kitchen equipment:

a teaspoon   *a tablespoon*

a dessertspoon   *a cup*

Other measurements are more specific:

For weight: *gram (g), kilogram (kg), ounce (oz), pound (lb)*

For liquids: *millilitre (ml), litres (l), fluid ounce (fl oz), pint (pt)*

Clear usage: 'about', 'around' and '....or so'

Abie uses some words and expressions which mean *not quite* or *not exactly*: '*around 225 grams of plain flour*' and '*about 30 grams*'. Here are some more words or expressions which mean *not exactly*:

Roughly 100 people live in that block of flats.

*It will take **approximately** 30 minutes to cook.*

*I should be **more or less** finished by 5pm.*

*The box is **almost** full.*

*There were **something like** 20 people who arrived late.*

I'd say they'll be more interested in the film than the book.

3 What words does Abie use to describe how she makes the pancakes? Use the verbs below to fill the gaps in what she says.

wait	heat	put	melt	flip	mix

1 .... some butter

2 .... them altogether

3 .... a pan

4 .... a little bit of butter in

5 .... for bubbles to form on the top of the mixture

6 .... the pancake over

Listening tip: intonation in lists

Listen to Abie's intonation (the sound of her voice) when she says what the children put on their pancakes:

'They cover their pancakes with maple syrup, or honey, or chocolate spread, or sometimes lemon and sugar.'

A speaker's intonation usually rises on each thing in a list, then falls on the last thing.

Part C

In this recording, Chris, an American living in the UK, talks about the food he likes to eat in both countries.

55

1 What ingredients does Chris mention? Tick (✓) the photos.

COBUILD CHECK: 'goes with'

If one thing **goes with** another thing it means they make each other better:

- The handsome scarf and hat that **went with** the suit.
- If there are words that **go with** a piece of music ...

2 Are these statements true or false? Put a tick (✓) to show the correct answer.

		True	False
1	Chris thinks the UK has great Mexican food.	....	....
2	Chris doesn't like Indian food at all.	....	....
3	Chris thinks that some people don't know what Mexican food is really like.	....	....
4	Chris thinks the most important thing about Mexican food is the spice.	....	....
5	Chris says that Mexican food is mostly meat and beans.	....	....

Useful vocabulary and phrases: adjectives that describe tastes

hot	*fresh*	*savoury*
bitter	*mild*	*stale*
bland	*rich*	*sour*
creamy	*salty*	*sweet*

---

3 Listen again and complete the gaps in what Chris says with words and phrases about food.

tastes	goes with	flavour	veggie	spices	fresh

1 There's a real depth of .... there.

2 It has to be very ....ingredients, a lot of bright ....

3 There are .... there but it's not about fire.

4 It's very .... -heavy.

5 it kind of .... a little bit of everything.

My review

I can recognize expressions of preference for meals and food types.	❏
I can follow descriptions of recipes including ingredients and quantities.	❏
I can understand words for describing food.	❏
I can understand descriptions of food cultures from different countries.	❏

17 GAMES AND SPORTS

Getting started

1 Which games or sports do you enjoy?
2 Why do you like them?
3 Do you prefer playing or watching?
4 How often do you play them?

Part A

In this recording, six people answer the question 'Which games or sports do you enjoy?'

56

Look at the pictures. Number the pictures in the order you hear them.

baseball

golf

football (UK)

running

squash

soccer (US)

> Speaker 2 describes sport as *huge* in her country. This means that sport is very popular there.
>
> Speaker 4 describes her sport as 'a *huge* favourite'. This means that she really enjoys this sport.

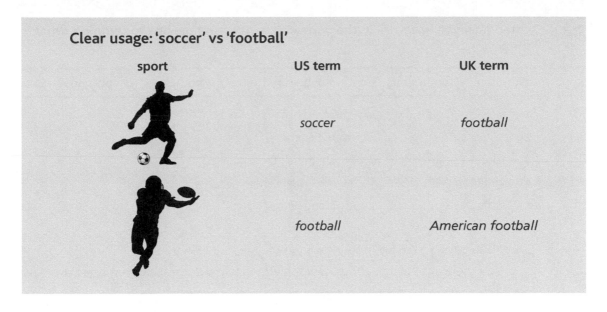

Clear usage: 'soccer' vs 'football'

sport	US term	UK term
	soccer	football
	football	American football

2 Listen again carefully to the six people. Fill in the table with ticks (✓) to show which information goes with each sport.

	plays twice a week	likes watching	plays with friends	played from age 4 or 5
soccer				
golf				
squash				
baseball				

Listening tip: focus on the question

When they are answering a question, people often give extra information. Sometimes this can help you to understand better. But try to stay focused on the *important* information while you listen.

Part B

Now listen to Hazel talking about a sport she enjoys playing.

1 Answer the questions to check your general understanding.

1 Hazel plays ...   **a** hockey   **b** golf

2 She likes ...   **a** playing alone   **b** playing in a team

3 She used to be a member of a ...   **a** club   **b** gym

4 She found going there ... **a** fun   **b** difficult

5 She prefers ...   **a** outdoor sports   **b** team sports

2 Listen again to Hazel. Fill in the gaps with words from the box to complete what she says.

like	interact	being	go	playing

1 I like .... team sports.

2 It's nice to .... with a team.

3 I found it quite difficult to motivate myself to ....

4 I kind of prefer .... in a team sport.

5 That's why I .... playing hockey.

> Hazel says 'you're just *sort of* having fun'.
>
> You use *sort of* to talk about how something is in a general, but not exact way.
>
> You may also hear *kind of*, which has the same meaning.

Part C

Now listen to a recording of Tim talking about a sport he enjoys watching.

Answer the questions to check your general understanding.

1 Tim's favourite sport is ...
  a rugby   **b** baseball   **c** hockey

2 The sport can be played by ...
  a tall players   **b** small players   **c** every kind of player

3 Tim watches a particular tournament ...
  a every week   **b** every year   **c** every four years

4 The tournament is called ...
  a Three Nations   **b** Six Nations   **c** Nine Nations

Useful vocabulary and phrases: physical descriptions

 tall   short

 thin   fat

 large   small

 strong   weak

 fast   slow

2 Listen again carefully to Tim. Fill in the gaps to check your detailed understanding.

variety	France	fat	thin	Italy	player	Ireland	Six

1 There's a place in rugby for every kind of ....

2 Tall, ... players; small, ... players ...

3 It means that you get, uh, a great .... of people who enjoy the sport.

4 The '........................ Nations' rugby tournament is an annual tournament.

5 Teams from England, ..., Scotland, Wales, ...

6 ... and, most recently joined, ...

> Tim says that rugby is a sport which 'generates great *team spirit*'.
>
> *Team spirit* is the feeling of pride and loyalty that makes players want their team to do well or to be the best.

3 Listen again to both Hazel and Tim's recordings. They both talk about being in a team. Listen for the expressions below and complete the table with a tick (✓) to show who says each one.

	Hazel	Tim
I like playing in a team		
working towards the same goal		
together as a team		
you get a great variety of, people who enjoy the sport		
it's nice to interact with a team		
come together in order to win a match		

COBUILD CHECK: variety

A **variety** of things is a number of different examples of the same thing.

• People change their mind for a **variety** of reasons.

• The university offers a wide **variety** of courses.

• They offer advice on a **variety** of topics.

My review

I can understand people talking about their favourite game or sport. ❏

I can understand why people enjoy particular games or sports. ❏

I can understand descriptions of sports players. ❏

I can listen for details about sports competitions. ❏

18 MUSIC AND FILMS

Getting started

1 What kind of music or films do you like?
2 Do you like popular, 'mainstream' music or films?
3 Or do you prefer something more unusual?
4 Do you like talking about music and films with your friends?

Part A

In this recording, six people talk about their favourite type of music or films.

59

① Look at the pictures and number them in the order you hear them.

Useful vocabulary and phrases: types of music and films

Music		Films	
blues	hip-hop	action	musical
classical	jazz	comedy	romance
country (and western)	rock	documentary	sci-fi
easy listening	R'n'B	family	thriller
electronic	pop	romcom	war
folk	world	horror	western

Part B

In this recording, Kerry and Kara talk about the type of films that they like. Kerry likes big 'blockbuster' films, but Kara likes smaller films.

60

1   What does Kerry like about blockbuster films and what does Kara like about smaller films? Choose your answers from the box below and write them under the correct heading.

> interesting stories   not about everyday life   glamorous
> actors earn a sensible amount of money   good acting   fun

Why Kerry likes blockbuster films

....

....

....

Why Kara likes smaller films

....

....

....

Kerry says 'I really like *blockbuster movies, mainstream movies*'.

- A *movie* is the American word for a *film*.
- A *blockbuster* is a film that is very popular and successful, usually because it is very exciting.
- A *mainstream movie* is a film that most people know or like.

2   Read the statements first, then play the recording. Are these statements true or false? Put a tick (✓) to show the correct answer.

		True	False
1	Kerry thinks good stories aren't important.	....	....
2	Kerry agrees that the acting in blockbusters is not good.	....	....
3	Kerry thinks that blockbuster movies are well made.	....	....
4	Kara says she prefers to talk about movies with her friends.	....	....
5	Kara says she likes to see movies that other people don't see.	....	....

3   Here are some expressions from the recording. Listen to them again in context and match them with their meaning on the right.

1	larger than life	**a**	to hate something
2	what (something) is about	**b**	the escape from everyday life
3	getting away from it all	**c**	something obvious and expected
4	can't stand	**d**	something bigger and more important than everyday things
5	so predictable	**e**	to fight back, and do the opposite of what most people do
6	rebel against	**f**	the real meaning or significance behind something

Part C

In this recording, Graham talks to Nikki about the music he loves. He describes the difference between 'big band' music and a more unusual style that was heard in smaller clubs.

1 Graham mentions six types of music. How many can you hear?

1 *swing music*   4 ....

2 ....   5 ....

3 ....   6 ....

> Graham talks about 'the more *underground* stuff'. You can use *underground* to describe something if it is unusual and is not popular or well known by most people.

2 Listen again to Graham and Nikki and answer the questions below.

1 What music is Graham listening to at the moment?
   a swing music   **b** dance music   **c** jazz music

2 When did that type of music start?
   a The 1920s   **b** The 1930s–40s   **c** The 1950s

3 How many horn-players did the big bands have?
   a 3 or 4   **b** 5   **c** maybe 10

4 How many horn-players did the smaller bands have?
   a 3 or 4   **b** 5   **c** maybe 10

5 Which one of these musicians played in small band?
   a Benny Goodman   **b** Glenn Miller   **c** Louis Jordan

6 Why does Graham think people liked the smaller clubs?
   a they liked to drink   **b** they were cheaper   **c** they liked to dance

7 What style of music was played in the smaller clubs?
   a underground   **b** jump blues   **c** rock 'n' roll

3 What adjectives do you hear for describing the music and musicians that Graham likes? Tick (✓) the words he uses.

rocking ....   amazing ....   superb ....

very hip ....   marvellous ....   unbelievably good ....

brilliant ....   fantastic ....   absolutely fantastic ....

great ....   really cool ....   absolutely wonderful ....

4   Look at the phrases below. Who says them: Graham or Nikki? Put a tick (✓) in the correct column.

	Graham	Nikki
1 There's a jazz night that we go to.	....	....
2 It loses the dance floor.	....	....
3 That's a great style of music to play.	....	....
4 My boyfriend's really into jazz.	....	....
5 What era does he like?	....	....
6 I like some of it.	....	....

> You can say you are *into* something to mean you are very interested in it. It is an informal expression.
>
> *My boyfriend's really into jazz.*

5   Read the statements first, then play the recording. Are these statements true or false? Put a tick (✓) to show the correct answer.

	True	False
1 Nikki's boyfriend loves jazz music.	....	....
2 Nikki loves all jazz music.	....	....
3 Graham thinks you can't dance to some jazz music .	....	....
4 They all like Ella Fitzgerald.	....	....
5 Graham goes to a jazz club in London.	....	....

Clear usage: 'lose'

Graham says that after the war, jazz '*loses* the dance floor'. He means that people stop dancing to it (because it has become complicated and hard to enjoy).

Nikki says her boyfriend 'just *loses himself* in' jazz music when he goes to the club. She means that he enjoys it a lot.

My review

I can recognize different types of music and films.	❑
I can follow people's likes and dislikes when talking about music and films.	❑
I can understand whether music or films are more popular or more unusual.	❑
I can follow discussions about why people like music or films.	❑

19 TRAVEL AND TOURISM

Getting started

1 Where did you go on your last trip?
2 Where would you like to go next?
3 What do you generally like to do on holiday?
4 How do you like to travel?

Part A

In this recording, six people talk about a place they visited, or would like to visit.

62

(1) Look at the pictures and number them in the order you hear them.

Tunisia

Greek Islands

Thailand

Maputo

Budapest

Washington DC

(2) Read this list of places. Now listen again to the six people. Underline the names of the places you hear.

1 America
2 Spain
3 Mozambique
4 Argentina
5 Sahara Desert

6 Santorini
7 Hong Kong
8 London
9 Paris
10 Budapest

Useful vocabulary and phrases: ways to travel

 walk
go / travel on foot

 cycle / bike
go / travel by bike

drive
go / travel in the car
take the car

 go / travel by taxi
take a taxi

 go / travel by bus
take the bus

 go / travel by train
take the train

 sail
go / travel by boat / ferry
take the boat / ferry

 fly
go by plane

Part B

Now listen to Lily talking about travel in Argentina.

63

Read the questions before you listen. Are these statements true or false?
Put a tick (✓) to show the correct answer.

		True	False
1	There are mountains in the south of the country.	....	....
2	Argentina is a beautiful country.	....	....
3	Argentina is a small country.	....	....
4	It is expensive to fly.	....	....
5	Most people travel by train.	....	....
6	Bus journeys can be very long.	....	....

Clear usage: 'have to' and 'can'

Lily says: 'you *have to* travel quite long distances'. You use *have to* when you are saying that someone must do something.

*You **have to** buy a ticket before you get on the train.*

She also says: 'you *can* fly'. If you *can* do something, you are able to do it or it is possible to do it.

*You **can** take a taxi from the airport.*

2 Listen again carefully. Match the items (on the left) with the word or phrase Lily uses to describe them (on the right).

1	landscape	**a**	quite long
2	places to visit	**b**	really beautiful
3	country	**c**	quite expensive
4	distances	**d**	sixteen or twenty hours long
5	flying	**e**	really beautiful
6	journeys	**f**	big

Clear usage: 'there's' vs 'there're'

Lily says: '*there's* mountains in the south'. You usually use *there's* [= *there is*] to talk about singular nouns and *there're* [= *there are*] to talk about plural nouns:

There're *mountains in the south.*

But in practice, English speakers often use *there's* instead of *there're*. You can do this too, but be careful to always use the correct form when writing.

Listening tip: repetition for emphasis

Lily uses the expression '*really beautiful*' twice. By using an expression more than once, the speaker is placing extra importance on that idea.

However, if you do this too often it could sound as though you just don't know how to say something a different way! So don't overuse the technique.

Part C

Now listen to Jen talking about where she likes to go and what she likes to do on holiday.

64

Which one of the three statements best represents her feelings about holidays?

a She likes to go to the mountains, especially to go skiing.

b She likes to go to the beach, but she also enjoys sightseeing in the city.

c She likes to go on long bus journeys and to visit new cities.

> Jen talks about being 'on *holiday*'. In the UK, a *holiday* is a period of time when you relax and enjoy yourself away from home. In the US, this is called a *vacation*.
>
> Jen also talks about having 'a week *off* work'. If you have time *off*, you do not go to work or school.

COBUILD CHECK: 'sightseeing'

If you go **sightseeing** or do some **sightseeing**, you travel around visiting the interesting places that tourists usually visit.

- During our vacation, we had a day's **sightseeing** in Venice.
- The hotel offers guided **sightseeing** tours.
- We spent the rest of the day shopping and **sightseeing**.

2 Now listen again and fill in the gaps in what Jen says.
Use the words in the box below.

| sightseeing | holiday | off | weekends | beach (×2) | day |

1 I like to relax when I'm on ....

2 I spend so much of my working .... in quite stressful situations.

3 I like to just get on a .... and lie on a ....

4 I also quite like having .... away to interesting places.

5 I quite like just having a couple of days of city or ....

6 If I have a week .... work, I like to sit on a beach.

> Jen mentions 'weekends away'. If you have a *weekend away*, you leave the place where you live and visit another place for a day or two at the weekend.

3 Jen says that she 'likes' some activities but that she only 'quite likes' others. Listen again to the recording and fill in the table with a tick (✓) below to show how Jen feels about each activity.

	to relax	to lie on a beach	weekends away	sightseeing	different activities	to read a book	to get a tan
likes							
quite likes							

My review

I can understand people talking about where they went on a trip. ☐
I can understand information about different ways of travelling. ☐
I can understand people talking about where they would like to go. ☐
I can understand people's attitudes about holiday activities. ☐

20 SHOPPING

Getting started

1 What kind of things do you like to go shopping for?
2 What do you like to buy online?
3 Where do you prefer to shop?
4 Do you prefer to shop in the high street or online?

Part A

In this recording, five people answer the question 'What do you like to buy online?'

🎧 65 **1** Look at the pictures, then listen to the recording. Number the pictures in the order you hear them.

holidays

clothes

music

groceries

books

2 Listen again to the five people talking about the things they buy online. Fill in the gaps with the word you hear in the recording. Use the words from exercise 1.

1 I love buying my .... online, buying the flights and booking the hotels.

2 I find it easier to buy .... online. I think you can get them delivered very conveniently.

3 I never buy CDs any more. I buy all my .... online.

4 I don't have time to go to the supermarket, so I buy all my .... online.

5 So I shop for .... a lot online, because when I go into stores I struggle to find clothes in my size.

COBUILD CHECK: 'online'

If you do something **online**, you do it using the Internet.

- I buy most of my clothes and shoes **online**.
- Users can view the map **online**.
- You can order tickets **online**.

Clear usage: 'shop for'

If you *shop for* something, you look for it before you buy it. You can visit stores or look online.

*I like **shopping for** clothes online.*

*I prefer to **shop for** clothes in department stores.*

Part B

Now listen to Catherine talking about her experience of shopping.

66

Choose the correct answer for each of the following questions.

1 Catherine likes to go shopping for ...

     a clothes   **b** books   **c** food

2 She likes to look round ...

     a supermarkets   **b** book shops   **c** department stores

3 Catherine says department stores have ...

     a everything in one place   **b** everything she wants   **c** everything you can imagine

4 She goes shopping ...

     a once a week   **b** once a month   **c** once a year

5 Catherine says she hates ...

     a crowded shops   **b** quiet shops   **c** large shops

> Catherine says she likes it when the store is *nicely laid out*. This means the store or the products on sale are arranged in an attractive way.

Useful vocabulary and phrases: clothes shopping

high street shopping	*department store*
online shopping	*changing room*
free delivery	*lighting*
logo	*good / bad customer service*

Listening tip: understanding conversations

- Don't try to understand every single word – just *listen* for key words.
- Use the information given in the exercises to help you.
- *Listen* several times – each time you listen, you might hear something new.

2 Listen again carefully to Catherine. She uses several adjectives. Fill the gaps to complete the sentences. Choose from the adjectives in the box.

careful	obvious	crowded	big	exhausting	fussy

1 It's not too .... looking round and seeing what you'd like to buy.

2 I'm really .... and .... about what I buy.

3 I really hate .... shops.

4 I'll often buy from the same companies, but I don't like it to be too ....

5 I don't like clothes which have got .... logos on them or things like that.

Part C

Genevieve and Fliss both live in London. Listen to their conversation about shopping. Genevieve starts the conversation by asking Fliss whether she prefers online or high street shopping.

67

Choose the correct answer for each of the following questions.

1 Fliss likes online shopping because it's ...
   a easier   **b** quicker   **c** cheaper

2 Fliss likes online shops that have ...
   a big discounts   **b** free delivery   **c** new clothes

3 Fliss thinks it's better to try clothes on ...
   a in a store   **b** in your own home   **c** with friends

4 Genevieve likes high street shopping because it's more ...
   a interesting   **b** expensive   **c** personal

5 Genevieve has experienced what type of customer service?
   a only good   **b** mostly good   **c** mostly bad

6 Genevieve thinks high street shopping is ...
   a busy and fun   **b** boring and dull   **c** relaxing

Genevieve and Fliss talk about shopping in the *high street*. In the UK, the *high street* of a town is the main street where most of the shops and banks are. *High street shopping* means shopping in large shops or stores in a town or city.

Clear usage: 'try on'

If you *try on* a piece of clothing, or if you *try* it *on*, you put it on in order to see if it fits you or if it looks nice.

Try on *the shoes to make sure they fit.*

---

2 Listen carefully again to Genevieve and Fliss. Choose the correct word to complete each phrase that they use.

1 So, do you prefer *city centre / high street / department store* shopping or online shopping?

2 I like *online / electronic / home* shopping more.

3 I do like online shopping, just because it's easier and I haven't got *money / time / energy* to shop all the time.

4 You get the customer service and you can *wear / buy / try on* your clothes.

5 Yeah, *sometimes / occasionally / often* bad, but the majority I've experienced is good.

6 You can try it on in your own home and you don't have to be in a squashed, hot *high street / department store / changing room.*

3 Listen again to Genevieve and Fliss. Use what you hear and the answers you gave for exercises 1 and 2 to help you decide if the descriptions are for online shopping or for high street shopping. Put a tick (✓) in the correct column.

	online shopping	high street shopping
1 easier	....	....
2 more personal experience	....	....
3 safer	....	....
4 takes less time	....	....
5 customer service	....	....
6 more fun	....	....
7 free delivery	....	....
8 can try on clothes at home	....	....
9 busy	....	....

My review

I can understand what things people like to shop for. ❏

I can understand language about differences between online and high street shopping. ❏

I can understand people's preferences about where they shop. ❏

MINI-DICTIONARY

Unit 1

age gap NOUN
a difference in age between two people • *There is a big age gap between me and my younger sister.*

close ADJECTIVE
near to something else • *The apartment is close to the beach.*

furthest ADVERB
most distant or remote from something • *I was sitting the furthest away from the stage, so I had trouble watching the concert.*

in particular PHRASE
especially • *Why did he notice her car in particular?*

personality NOUN
the qualities that make you different from other people • *She has such a kind, friendly personality.*

talkative ADJECTIVE
talking a great deal • *John got nervous and became talkative.*

twin NOUN
one of two people who were born at the same time to the same mother • *Sarah was looking after the twins.*

Unit 2

be the case PHRASE
used to say that something happens or is happening • *It's raining outside, and I've forgotten my umbrella, as is often the case.*

clinic NOUN
a place where people receive medical advice or treatment • *My father's doctor in a clinic.*

journalist NOUN
a person whose job is to collect news stories and write about them for newspapers, magazines, television or radio • *The president spoke to an audience of two hundred journalists.*

programme NOUN
a television or radio show • *I was watching my favourite programme on television.*

running late PHRASE
unlikely to get somewhere on time • *I was running late for school.*

shave NOUN
the act of removing hair from your face or body by cutting it off using a special knife or a piece of electric equipment • *I had a shave this morning.*

skip VERB
to decide not to do something that you usually do • *Don't skip breakfast.*

walk NOUN
a trip that you make by walking, usually for pleasure • *I went for a walk after lunch.*

Unit 3

bungalow NOUN
a house that has only one level, and no stairs • *I live in a bungalow, and my bedroom is right next to the kitchen.*

creature NOUN
a living thing that is not a plant • *Like all living creatures, birds need plenty of water.*

dinner NOUN
the main meal of the day, usually served in the evening • *Would you like to stay and have dinner?*

edge NOUN
the part of something that is farthest from the middle • *We lived in a block of flats on the edge of town.*

gear NOUN
the equipment or special clothing that you use for a particular activity • *He took his fishing gear with him.*

middle NOUN
the part of something that is furthest from the edges • *Howard stood in the middle of the room.*

survive VERB
to still exist after a difficult or dangerous time • *It's a miracle that anyone survived.*

upstairs NOUN
the floor or floors of a building that are higher than the ground floor • *This house doesn't have an upstairs.*

downstairs NOUN
a lower or ground floor • *I live in the downstairs of this building.*

wildlife NOUN
used for talking about the animals and other living things that live in nature • *The area is rich in wildlife.*

Unit 4

boss NOUN
the person in charge of you at the place where you work • *He likes his new boss.*

career NOUN
a job that you do for a long time, or the years of your life that you spend working • *She had a long career as a teacher.*

change NOUN
an occasion when something becomes different • *There will soon be some big changes in our company.*

juggle VERB
to try to give enough time or attention to lots of different things • *Mike juggled a family of 11 with a career as a journalist.*

lawyer NOUN
a person whose job is to advise people about the law and to represent them in court • *His lawyers say that he is not guilty.*

Unit 5

begrudge VERB
to feel angry towards someone because you feel they don't have the right to do or say something • *I begrudge you for criticizing my outfit.*

couch NOUN
a long, comfortable seat for two or three people • *We all sat together on the couch and watched a film.*

current ADJECTIVE
happening now • *The current situation is different from the one in 1990.*

expatriate NOUN
someone who is living in a country other than the one where they were born • *I'm an Australian expatriate living in Vietnam.*

judge VERB
to form an opinion about someone or something • *People should wait, and judge the film when they see it for themselves.*

special occasion NOUN
an important event, ceremony, or celebration • *This shop sells beautiful dresses for special occasions.*

tempting ADJECTIVE
attractive • *The berries look tempting to children, but they're poisonous.*

weird ADJECTIVE
strange • *He's a very weird guy.*

Unit 6

aspect NOUN
a quality or a part of something • *He was interested in all aspects of the work here.*

background NOUN
the type of family you come from and the type of education and experiences you have had • *He came from a very poor background.*

chat NOUN
an informal and friendly chat • *I had a chat with my friend John.*

clean up PHRASE
to clean a place completely • *Who is going to clean up this mess?*

cleaner NOUN
a person whose job is to clean the rooms and furniture inside a building • *This is the hospital where Sid worked as a cleaner.*

distribution NOUN
when you give out something in shares • *Make sure there's a fair distribution of sweets at the party.*

pet NOUN
an animal that you keep in your home • *Do you have any pets?*

terraced house NOUN
one of a row of houses that are joined together by both of their side walls • *My family has just moved into a terraced house.*

washing-up NOUN
when you wash the plates, cups and other things that you have used for cooking and eating a meal • *Martha offered to do the washing-up.*

Unit 7

corner shop NOUN
a small shop, usually on the corner of a street, that sells mainly food and household goods • *I'm going to the corner shop to buy some milk.*

exhibition NOUN
a public event where art or interesting objects are shown • *The museum has an exhibition of photographs.*

explore VERB
to travel around a place to find out what it is like • *The best way to explore the area is in a boat.*

green space NOUN
land covered by trees or grass in a town or city • *I wish there was more green space in my neighbourhood.*

incredible ADJECTIVE
used for saying how good something is, or to make what you are saying stronger • *The food was incredible.*

kitchenware NOUN
pots and pans, knives, forks, spoons, and other tools or objects used in the kitchen • *I need some kitchenware for my new flat.*

plan VERB
to decide in detail what you are going to do • *He plans to leave Baghdad on Monday.*

stuff NOUN
things in general • *There is a huge amount of useful stuff on the Internet.*

vibrant ADJECTIVE
full of energy and enthusiasm • *She has a vibrant personality.*

Unit 8

coast NOUN
the land that is next to the sea • *We stayed at a camp site on the coast.*

fiesta NOUN
a time of public entertainment and parties • *The town is having a fiesta on the beach.*

guest house NOUN
a small hotel • *I think we'll stay in a guest house when we go to Paris.*

harbour NOUN
an area of water next to the land where boats can safely stay • *The fishing boats left the harbour and went out to sea.*

horizon NOUN
the line that appears between the sky and the land or the sea • *A small boat appeared on the horizon.*

ideal NOUN
a principle or idea that people try to achieve • *We must defend the ideals of liberty and freedom.*

miss VERB
to feel sad because someone is no longer with you, or because you no longer have the thing • *Your mother and I are going to miss you at Christmas.*

rhythm NOUN
a regular series of sounds, movements, or actions • *His body moved to the rhythm of the music.*

surrounded ADJECTIVE
having something all around you • *I was surrounded by children at the park.*

typical ADJECTIVE
used for describing a good example of a type of person or thing • *Tell me about your typical day.*

Unit 9

A levels PLURAL NOUN
British qualifications that people take when they are seventeen or eighteen years old • *Laura is taking her A levels next summer.*

boarding school NOUN
a school where the pupils live during the term • *Now she is away at boarding school.*

flight NOUN
a trip in an aircraft • *The flight to Sydney will take eight hours.*

homesick ADJECTIVE
feeling unhappy because you are away from home and missing your family and friends • *He was homesick for his family.*

identity NOUN
the characteristics of a person or place that make them different from others • *I wanted a sense of my own identity.*

strict ADJECTIVE
expecting rules to be obeyed and people to behave properly • *My parents were very strict.*

warm ADJECTIVE
friendly • *She was a warm and loving mother.*

Unit 10

change VERB
to get off one bus, train or plane, and get on to another in order to continue your journey • *I changed planes in Chicago.*

closest ADJECTIVE
nearest • *It's the closest house to the beach.*

concrete NOUN
a hard substance made by mixing a grey powder with sand and water • *We sat on the concrete floor.*

confirm VERB
to assert for a second or further time, so as to make more firm and clear • *He confirmed that he would appear in court.*

customs NOUN
the place at an airport, for example, where people have to show certain goods that they have bought abroad • *He walked through customs.*

luggage NOUN
the bags that you take with you when you travel • *Do you have any luggage?*

obviously ADVERB
used for stating something that you expect your listener to know already • *Obviously I'll be disappointed if I don't get the job.*

rather ADVERB
more willingly • *Kids would rather play than study.*

Unit 11

B.A. NOUN
a first degree in an arts or social science subject. B.A. is an abbreviation for 'Bachelor of Arts' • *I graduated with a B.A. in History.*

break NOUN
a short period of time when you have a rest • *We get a 15-minute break for coffee.*

come up with PHRASE
to produce or find something • *I came up with an idea for a story!*

demanding ADJECTIVE
requiring a lot of time, energy, or attention • *My new job is demanding.*

grade VERB
to judge the quality of something • *Restaurants are graded according to the quality of the food and service.*

harshly ADVERB
in a way that is hard and unkind • *He was harshly treated in prison.*

initially ADVERB
near the beginning of a process or situation • *The list initially included 11 players.*

Masters NOUN
a university degree which is of a higher level than a first degree and usually takes one or two years to complete • *I did my Masters in Geography at the University of Edinburgh.*

routine NOUN
the usual activities that you do every day • *The players changed their daily routine.*

theology NOUN
the study of religion and the nature of God • *I studied theology for four years at university.*

Unit 12

candidate NOUN
someone who is trying to get a particular job, or trying to win a political position • *He is a candidate for the job.*

charity NOUN
an organization that collects money for people who need help • *Michael is working for a children's charity.*

graduate NOUN
a student who has completed a course at a college or university • *His parents are both college graduates. They studied at Cornell.*

handshake NOUN
when you take someone's right hand with your own right hand and move it up and down as a way of greeting them or showing that you have agreed about something • *He has a strong handshake.*

motivate VERB
to make someone feel determined to do something • *How do you motivate people to work hard?*

position NOUN
a job in a company or an organization • *He left a career in teaching to take a position with IBM.*

sector NOUN
a particular part of something, especially of a society or an economy • *The manufacturing sector is expanding steadily.*

unemployment NOUN
when people who want to work cannot work, because there are not enough jobs • *Robert's family live in an area of high unemployment.*

willing ADJECTIVE
happy to do something • *He was a natural and willing learner.*

work experience NOUN
a short period spent in a workplace, usually by young people, to learn what it is like to do that kind of work • *My friend is doing work experience at a publishing company.*

Unit 13

communication NOUN
the act of giving information to someone, for example by speaking, writing, or sending radio signals • *Communication is important in a relationship.*

distraction NOUN
something that turns your attention away from something else that you want to concentrate on • *Mobile phones in cars are a dangerous distraction for drivers.*

effectively ADVERB
in a way that produces the results that you want • *We always work effectively together.*

errand NOUN
a short trip to do a job or to buy something • *I did an errand for her when she was ill.*

face to face ADVERB
meeting someone and talking to them directly • *I need to discuss this project face to face with my teacher.*

interact VERB
the way that two people or things communicate or work in relation to each other • *At birth, you become a social being, interacting with others.*

motivated ADJECTIVE
determined • *We are looking for a highly motivated and hard-working professional.*

relaxed ADJECTIVE
to feel more calm and less worried • *I felt relaxed when I got back from my holiday in Spain.*

remote access NOUN
a system which allows you to gain access to a particular computer or network using a separate computer • *Can I get remote access to my husband's phone from my computer?*

self-disciplined ADJECTIVE
having the power to discipline yourself to work or study hard • *You need to be very self-disciplined at university.*

Unit 14

complain VERB
to say that you are not satisfied with someone or something • *I shouldn't complain; I've got a good job.*

cut down PHRASE
to use or do less of something • *He cut down on coffee.*

entitled ADJECTIVE
to be allowed to have or do something • *They are entitled to first class travel.*

finance NOUN
money, or the activity of managing large amounts of money • *Professor Buckley teaches finance at Princeton University.*

hurried ADJECTIVE
rushed • *I woke up late this morning so I had a rushed breakfast.*

look after PHRASE
to take care of someone • *Maria looks after the kids while I'm at work.*

pension NOUN
money that you regularly receive from a business or the government after you stop working because of your age • *He gets a £35,000-a-year pension.*

youth hostel NOUN
a place where people can stay cheaply when they are travelling • *My friends and I are staying in a youth hostel in Milan.*

Unit 15

gonna VERB
an informal way of saying 'going to' • *What am I gonna do?*

home NOUN
the house or flat where someone lives • *Hi, Mum, I'm home!*

metal NOUN
a hard substance such as iron, steel or gold • *All of the houses had metal roofs.*

nightlife NOUN
social life or entertainment taking place in the late evening or night, as in nightclubs • *It's a university town, with lots of nightlife.*

on the planet PHRASE
used to emphasize that something is the best, worst, etc. • *New York City is the best city on the planet!*

real estate NOUN
the business of selling houses, buildings and land • *It was a friend of his father's who had helped him start in real estate.*

residential ADJECTIVE
containing houses rather than offices or shops • *We drove through a residential area of Birmingham.*

upload VERB
to move a document or a program from your computer to another one, using the Internet • *Next, upload the files on to your website.*

work VERB
to operate correctly • *My mobile phone isn't working.*

Unit 16

assumption NOUN
something that is supposed to be true, sometimes wrongly • *Their assumption is that all men and women think alike.*

bubbles PLURAL NOUN
small balls of air or gas in a liquid • *Air bubbles rise to the surface.*

gorge on VERB
to eat lots of something in a greedy way • *We gorged on some delicious Mexican food last night.*

hands down PHRASE
easily • *My favourite movie hands down is Avatar.*

-heavy COMBINING FORM having large quantities of a certain thing • *This menu is very pasta-heavy.*

ingredients PLURAL NOUN
the things that you use to make something, especially when you are cooking • *Mix together all the ingredients.*

recipe NOUN
a list of food and a set of instructions telling you how to cook something • *Do you have a recipe for chocolate cake?*

trade-off NOUN
a situation where you make a compromise between two things, or where you exchange all or part of one thing for another • *There is often a trade-off between eating healthy and saving money.*

Unit 17

allegiance NOUN
support for and loyalty to a group, person, or belief • *His allegiance to his country of birth was strong.*

annual ADJECTIVE
happening once every year • *They held their annual meeting on 20th May.*

huge ADJECTIVE
an informal word for 'popular' • *Partying is huge among teenagers.*

interact VERB
the way that two people or things communicate or work in relation to each other • *At birth, you become a social being, interacting with others.*

motivate VERB
to make someone feel determined to do something • *How do you motivate people to work hard?*

root for VERB
to give someone support while they are doing something difficult or trying to defeat another person • *I'm not rooting for any team in particular.*

season NOUN
a time each year when something happens • *The football season begins again soon.*

socialize VERB
to meet other people socially, for example at parties • *I like socializing and making new friends.*

tournament NOUN
a sports competition in which each player who wins a game plays another game, until just one person or team remains • *Tiger Woods won the tournament in 2000.*

triathlon NOUN
an athletics competition in which each competitor takes part in three events: swimming, cycling, and running • *Alistair Brownlee won the men's triathlon at the London Olympics.*

Unit 18

big band NOUN
a musical style in which a large group of musicians who play jazz or dance music • *I love big band music.*

develop from VERB
to follow as a result of something else • *Her cough had developed from smoking too much.*

escapist ADJECTIVE
making people think about pleasant or unlikely things instead of the uninteresting or unpleasant aspects of their life • *Reading fiction is a great form of escapist entertainment.*

glamour NOUN
quality of being more attractive, exciting, or interesting than ordinary people or things • *He loved the glamour of Hollywood.*

guarantee NOUN
a promise • *He gave me a guarantee he would finish the job.*

hardcore ADJECTIVE
extreme • *Some rock n' roll fans are hardcore.*

horns NOUN
a musical wind instruments • *The Nocturne was beautifully played by the horns.*

instrument NOUN
an object that you use for making music • *Tim plays four musical instruments, including piano and guitar.*

preclude VERB
to prevent something from happening or being included • *At 84, John feels his age precludes too much travel.*

speak-easy NOUN
a place where people could buy alcoholic drinks illegally in the United States between 1920 and 1933, when alcohol was forbidden • *My grandmother remembers going to speak-easies.*

talented ADJECTIVE
having a natural ability to do something well • *Howard is a talented pianist.*

Unit 19

bathhouse NOUN
a public or private building containing baths and often other facilities such as a sauna • *After a busy week, I like to visit the local bathhouse to relax.*

camel NOUN
an animal with one or two large lumps on its back • *We saw some camels at the zoo.*

distance NOUN
the amount of space between two places • *Measure the distance between the wall and the table.*

export NOUN
a product that one country sells to another country • *Spain's main export is oil.*

journey NOUN
an occasion when you travel from one place to another • *Their journey took them from Paris to Brussels.*

landscape NOUN
everything you can see when you look across an area of land • *We travelled through the beautiful landscape of northern Scotland.*

stressful ADJECTIVE
making you feel worried or upset • *She's got a very stressful job.*

tan NOUN
when your skin has become darker because you have spent time in the sun • *She is tall and blonde, with a tan.*

Unit 20

conveniently ADVERB
in a way that is suitable for one's purpose or needs • *My mum conveniently drove me to the party.*

crowded ADJECTIVE
full of people • *He looked slowly around the small crowded room.*

customer service NOUN
the way that companies behave towards their customers, for example how well they treat them • *This mail-order business has very good customer service.*

display VERB
to put something in a place where people can see it • *Old soldiers proudly displayed their medals.*

don't get me wrong PHRASE
a phrase used when you want to make sure someone doesn't misunderstand you • *Don't get me wrong! I think she's a lovely person, but she can be a bit rude sometimes.*

get a feel for PHRASE
to become familiar with something • *I wanted to visit the city to get a feel for it.*

fussy ADJECTIVE
very difficult to please and interested in small details • *She is very fussy about her food.*

size NOUN
one of a series of particular measurements for clothes and shoes • *What size are your feet?*

squashed ADJECTIVE
put or pushed into a place where there is not enough room • *I felt squashed in that lift because I was with ten other people!*

struggle VERB
to try hard to do something that you find very difficult • *She struggled to find the right words.*

Unit 1   Family life

A
1

B
1

twin sister

•Durham

brother

London •
Boscombe • •Salisbury
© Collins Bartholomew Ltd 2012

older sister

2

1 a   2 c   3 b   4 c   5 b

3

1 I live quite <u>close</u> to my brother – he lives in London <u>as well</u>.
2 My twin sister lives in Durham so she's <u>several hours away</u> on the train.
3 We try and meet up when we can especially Christmas and Easter so <u>holiday times</u>, really.
4 When we meet up we'll play tennis or squash and hockey <u>in particular</u>, really.
5 We try and <u>make excuses</u> to meet up still.

C
1

1 F   2 F   3 T   4 F   5 T

2

1 two   3 on   5 like
2 older   4 school   6 languages

3

	lives in the north of England	sees Lily once a year	makes Lily laugh	likes teaching	lives in London	lives in India
Lily				✓	✓	
Lily's mum	✓					
Lily's dad		✓				✓
Lily's sister	✓		✓	✓		

Unit 2   Daily Life

A
1

1 b   2 b   3 a   4 c   5 c

B
1

3   5   1

6
4
2

2

1 do   3 eat   5 check
2 jump, have   4 head off

C

1

1 T   2 F   3 T   4 T   5 F

2

1 b   2 d   3 a   4 c

D

1

1 b   2 a   3 b   4 b   5 a

2

	has breakfast	watches TV	gets up	goes to bed	makes dinner	has a shower
before work		✓	✓		✓	✓
after work	✓			✓		

Unit 3   Childhood

A

1

5
3
1
4
2

2

1 I was <u>brought up</u> in the countryside.

2 <u>When I was</u> five years old I learned to ride a bike. and my dad, every weekend, <u>would take</u> me round the block on it.

3 Myself and my brother <u>would go</u> to the sweet shop and we <u>would spend</u> our 50 pence.

4 The house I <u>grew up</u> in was on the same street as the library [...] I <u>used to</u> spend all my time reading.

5 During my childhood I <u>spent</u> every weekend at the beach.

B

1

different ✓
crazy
brilliant ✓
happy ✓
healthy ✓
great ✓
lively
interesting ✓
OK
colourful ✓

2

1 in the countryside / (the middle of) North Carolina

2 camping, hiking, hunting, and fishing

3 fishing gear, pellet gun, and a backpack

4 snakes and crayfish / various creatures

5 12

6 Yes

3

1 outside   3 contrast   5 lifestyle
2 escape   4 effort   6 opportunity

C

1

...a bungalow...   ....a garden.....   ....flats.......

.....a family..... .....swings...... .....markets..... ......clothes..... ...vegetables... ....fish.......

2

1	F	3	F	5	F	7	T
2	T	4	F	6	T		

3

1	big	4	beautiful	7	lovely
2	little	5	big		
3	little	6	wonderful		

Unit 4   Life changes

1

wedding 3   children 2   new job 1   moving abroad 5   leaving home 4

1

1	F	2	T	3	F	4	T	5	F	6	T

2

1   …before I had <u>children</u> my work was <u>everything</u> to me.

2   When I had the children although my work was still very <u>important</u> to me,

3   I think my <u>priorities</u> changed and I started to see things in a <u>different</u> way.

4   It's been <u>difficult</u> to juggle and balance out work and home life.

5   I think now I try to put things in balance and not take things too <u>seriously</u>.

3

1   every spare moment

2   furthering my <u>career</u>

3   my <u>priorities</u> changed

4   see things in a <u>different</u> way

5   put things in <u>balance</u>

6   let things get <u>out</u> of <u>perspective</u>

1

it took up a lot of my time ......2......

I went back to university ......5......

to write books part time ......4......

I'm my own boss ......7......

I wanted to make a change ......3......

five or six years ago ......1......

now I write books ......6......

2

1	a	5	b
2	a	6	c
3	b	7	c
4	a		

3

1	weekends	4	creative
2	part-time	5	successful
3	degree		

Unit 5   Your friends

A

1

Which speakers talk about ...	Genevieve	Fliss	Jeremy	Catherine	Laura	Chris
their friends from university?	✓	✓				
their friends from primary school (ages 5–11)?	✓	✓				
seeing their friends at the weekends?			✓		✓	
friends that live in other countries?			✓	✓		
having one 'best' friend?		✓				✓
talking to their friends online?			✓			✓
friends being important to them?	✓	✓	✓	✓	✓	✓

2

1   It'd be a very <u>lonely lonely</u> world if you didn't have someone outside of your family to <u>communicate with</u>.

2   People kind of <u>come and go</u> in your lives but there are always certain people that stay.

3   It's good to have people you can relate to and <u>catch up with</u>.

4   I don't <u>see</u> them very often but when we do see each other it's like <u>no time</u> has passed.

5   I feel very <u>lucky</u> to have such a wonderful group of <u>girlfriends</u>.

6   I try to <u>spend time with</u> friends because I think it's important to <u>keep in contact</u>.

B

1

catch up with	.2.
spend (a lot of) time with	.3.
modern technology	.6.
keep in touch	.1.
international friends	.5.
keep in contact with	.7.
hang out	.4.

2

1   text ✓ phone ✓

2   go to see bands ✓ go for meals ✓

3   France ✓ America ✓

4   Twitter ✓ Facebook ✓

C

1

being honest	.1.
giving advice and listening	.2.
giving each other time on their own	.3.

2

1   Before I leave the house […] I'll go up to your room, just to <u>get your opinion</u> on what I'm wearing.

2   That's what's really good about having such a <u>close</u> friend, is because you can <u>be honest</u> with me.

3   I go to you for advice a lot because I know I can <u>trust you</u> and hopefully I can give you <u>useful advice</u> as well.

4   It's sort of important we <u>make time</u> for each other but we also make time for <u>ourselves</u>.

5   We're very good at judging when you might want your <u>own space</u> and when you might want to <u>spend time with</u> friends.

6   I know it is important not to be on top of <u>each other</u> all the time.

Unit 6   Your house

A

1

4

1

5

2

3

B

1

1 b   2 b   3 a   4 a

2

cleaning up the kitchen	making new friends	having people around	having a chat	when you just want to hang out	hanging the washing out
	✓	✓	✓	✓	

3

1 chores   3 communication   5 friends
2 cultures   4 hang

4

1 c   3 d   4 a   5 e   6 b

C

1

1 T   2 F   3 F   4 T   5 F   6 T

2

1 I do the cooking
2 he does the cooking
3 he'd only cleaned the bathroom once
4 she never cleans up the kitchen
5 I said it wasn't acceptable
6 now we don't argue

3

	hanging out the washing	cleaning up the kitchen	doing the cooking	using the washing machine	cleaning the bathroom
Sarah	✓	✓		✓	
Ana		✓	✓		✓

Unit 7   Life in the city

A

1

1 b   2 a   3 a   4 b

2

1 lots   2 lots   3 little   4 many

B

1

1 a   2 b   3 a   4 a

2

	GOOD	BAD
incredible	✓	
not that great		✓
awful		✓
fantastic	✓	

C

1

likes: coffee shops, restaurants, meeting new people
dislikes: noise, cost of living

2

1 coffee shops, restaurants
2 friends, people
3 noise
4 cost of life

D

1

 3
 4
 5
 2
 1

2

1 T   2 F   3 T   4 F   5 T   6 T

3

Yes: fresh fish, mobile phones, clothes, kitchenware
No: lunch, breakfast, furniture

Unit 8   Life in the countryside

 A
1

1   4   3   2   5

B

1

quiet ✓	friendly people ✓
clean air ✓	hiking ✓
lots to do evenings	beautiful views ✓
horse-riding ✓	nice food
going to the sea ✓	trees

3
1 The <u>air's</u> really clean.
2 <u>There are</u> beautiful views.
3 The <u>people are</u> friendly.
4 <u>There's</u> less to do in the evenings.
5 <u>It's</u> the ideal place to go.

2
1 near   4 evenings   7 holiday
2 coast   5 outdoor
3 horizon   6 ideal

C

1

beach   river   countryside   tourists   hotels   harbour

2
1 F   2 F   3 T   4 F   5 T

3

nature	trees
the sea	birds (birds singing)

4
1 You really <u>miss</u> [d]
2 I took it for <u>granted</u> [a]
3 you <u>don't see</u> that every day [b]
4 but it makes you <u>appreciate it</u> more [c]

Unit 9   Living in another country

 A

	Country or city?	How long
1	Japan	1 year
2	Hong Kong	10 years
3	Argentina	6 months
4	Germany	5 years
5	London	5 years

B

1
1 17   3 1   5 620
2 36   4 8 and 10

2
1 F   2 T   3 F   4 T   5 F

3

 I went to <u>school</u> there.

 I learned to speak another <u>language</u>.

 I got to know another <u>culture</u>.

 I lived with a <u>family</u>.

 I didn't get very <u>homesick</u>.

C

1

| 1 | b | 2 | b | 3 | a | 4 | a | 5 | b |

2

1 go travelling
2 friends of friends
3 teaching English
4 whole year
5 very different

3

Celia's time in Japan made her think about Japanese and English <u>culture</u> and also about who she was – her <u>identity</u>. She began to <u>appreciate</u> her own English family more. Her Japanese host parents were very <u>strict</u> and didn't allow their children much <u>freedom</u> or <u>independence</u>.

Unit 10   Getting around

A

1

......cinema.....   ..sports ground   ....hospital...

......hotel.......   Apollo Theatre.

2

a   2
b   7
c   4
d   5
e   6
f   1
g   8
h   3

3

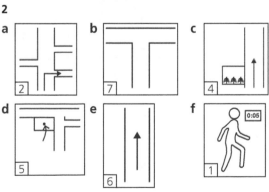

4

1 The Apollo Theatre is about <u>seven hundred</u> metres away.
2 The cinema is called <u>Riverside</u> Studios.
3 The hospital is a big <u>grey</u> building.
4 The hotel is on a road called <u>Shortlands</u>.
5 You can get to the sports ground by <u>bus</u>.

1

2
1 a 2 b 3 c 4 a 5 c 6 c 7 b
3
Piccadilly, Hammersmith, bus station, shopping centre, ten, right, left, fourth, hospital, second

---

Unit 11   Studying and learning

A
1

2
1 e   2 d   3 a   4 c   5 b

B
1
1 a   2 b   3 b   4 b   5 a
2
| 1 | doing | 3 | offer | 5 | learn |
| 2 | attended | 4 | did | 6 | working |

3

Name:	Kerry
University:	Oxford
Course of study:	MBA
Number of months:	12

C
1
1 T   2 F   3 T   4 F   5 T   6 F
2
1 c   2 a   3 d   4 b
3
1 playing
2 taking
3 trying
4 learn
5 get together

Unit 12   Starting work

A
1

- I was sixteen years old   .2.
- about 8 weeks   .4.
- I hated the whole job   .5.

- I worked in a toy store   .1.
- about $5.50 an hour   .3.

2

What was your first job?	How old were you?	How much were you paid?	How long did you spend there?	Did you enjoy it?
Smoked salmon factory	16	£3.50	1 day	No
toy store	✗	$5.85 an hour	2 years	Yes
photographic kiosk	17	✗	✗	Yes
fast food restaurant	16	£3.50 an hour	8 weeks	No
expensive restaurant	16	£5 an hour	1.5 years	No

B

1

1 What qualifications do you have? .2.

2 Do you have a valid driving licence? .6.

3 What experience do you have that is relevant for this role? .1.

4 And can you tell me what you know about the company already? .4.

5 Have you worked in a similar job before? .3.

6 Are you able to work in the evenings or the weekends? .5.

2

1 d   2 e   3 a   4 f   5 b   6 c

C

1

communication skills (✓)   experience (✓)

technical skills ( )   driving licence ( )

research (✓)   qualifications ( )

dressing smartly (✓)   handshake (✓)

2

1 It's a <u>junior</u> position within a sales team.

2 I'm looking for somebody who is a good <u>communicator</u>.

3 Somebody who gets on with people, and also is willing to <u>learn</u>.

4 Somebody who's thought about the company that they're going to work for, so they've done some <u>research</u>.

5 <u>Experience</u> is important when you're employing somebody.

6 When a candidate turns up, first impressions do count, so it's important to think about how <u>you're dressed</u>.

7 Dressing <u>smartly</u> gives a good impression.

8 A handshake is very important 'cause it gives a <u>positive</u> impression.

D

1

1 F   2 T   3 F   4 T   5 T

2

1 1 agencies; websites

2 lots of experience

3 have an updated CV; be disciplined with yourself

4 a lot of unemployment; not being organized

3

1 I don't need to <u>look for</u> very long in order to get a job.

2 I <u>have</u> seven years of work experience.

3 If a job <u>comes up</u> in that sector I have a good chance of getting it.

4 … depending on which job I'm <u>applying for</u>.

5 <u>Looking for</u> a job can be quite hard.

6 So you <u>have to</u> be very disciplined.

7 <u>Make sure</u> that you're applying every single day.

Unit 13   Working from home

A

1

4   2   3   1

2

1 (their) homework

2 technical documents

3 menus and food

4 chairs, cupboards and cabinets

1

How long?	Why?	Job	Good points	Bad points	Does she enjoy it?
A few years	Because she has children to take to school	Writer	No long commute, the day goes quickly	It can be lonely, no fresh air	Yes

2

1   commute   3   stuck   5   racing through
2   set up   4   pick up   6   productive

3

1   ... it suits me very well <u>because</u> I've small children, <u>so</u> I have to take them to school.

2   ... working from home <u>means</u> I'm nearer to their school.

3   I'm a writer <u>so</u> it's quite easy for me to work from home.

4   ... go to the shop and buy something small <u>just to</u> get out of the house.

5   <u>'cause</u> you feel a bit stuck at your desk otherwise.

6   But often the day goes very quickly <u>because</u> I'm racing through the work.

7   ... you have to be quite self-disciplined <u>in that</u> you're the one that makes yourself ...

C

1

	Abie	Dave
They work from home every day.	✓	
It takes a long time to get to work/the city.		✓
They use a computer for work.	✓	✓
They stay in touch with work during the day.		✓
They like to see people during the day.	✓	✓
They prefer to work at home all the time.	✓	

2

1   provides   3   access   5   do
2   connect into   4   keep up with   6   rely on

3

1   I work from home, uh, *because* <u>I live quite far from my office</u>.

2   It's about an hour's drive, *so* <u>my company provides remote access</u>.

3   It's good *'cause* <u>it's a lot more relaxed</u>.

4   I do miss being able to just go up to someone and ask a question, *because* <u>you kind of rely on email</u>.

5   It can be hard to stay motivated, just *because* <u>there's a lot more distractions</u> so <u>I don't know if I could work from home all the time</u>.

4

1   T   2   F   3   F   4   F

Unit 14   Your career

A

1

1   b   2   a   3   b   4   a   5   a   6   a

2

1   worked   3   help   5   would
2   decided, wanted   4   like   6   continue

3

1   in the past ( )   5   a lot of hours (✓)
2   in the future (✓)   6   a few hours ( )
3   for four years (✓)   7   all the time (✓)
4   for many years ( )   8   at the moment (✓)

B

1

1   b

2

Hazel: demanding, busy
Patrick: pleasant, stressful, demanding

3

1   face to face   3   deal with   5   requested
2   stressful   4   happy   6   complain

C

1

1   T   2   F   3   F   4   T

2

1   g   2   h   3   e   4   a   5   b   6   c   7   d   8   f

3

1   I'm not far off retirement now.

2   I could take a pension now. I'm entitled to one.

3   There may not even be any work come September.
4   Universities are cutting down on the staff.
5   It might be a forced retirement!

6   But I don't mind, really.
7   It'll be nice just to have a less hurried life.
8   A little bit more of the things you want.

Unit 15   Your future

(A)

1

1   b   2   b   3   b   4   c   5   a   6   b

2

1   c   2   e   3   a   4   f   5   d   6   b

3

Current job: 2, 6, 8, 9
Ideal job: 1, 3, 4, 5, 7

4

1   move   4   be
2   like   5   be
3   work   6   feel

(B)

1

1   T   2   F   3   T   4   T   5   F   6   F   7   T

2

1   travel   3   blogging   5   Islands   7   talk
2   share   4   like   6   post   8   better

3

1   to get paid   .b.   4   hype   .e.
2   professional   .c.   5   relate to one person .a.
3   get caught up in   .d.   6   post   .f.

4

the nightlife, the beaches, places she's been, places she
ate in, photos

Unit 16   Food

(A)

1

....fruit....   ...pasta...   ..chicken..   ..curry....

(B)

1

milk (✓)   jam   sugar (✓)   bread   butter (✓)

lemon (✓) flour (✓) baking powder cheese   eggs (✓)
                              (✓)

2

1   <u>225</u> grams of plain flour
2   <u>a tablespoon</u> or so of baking powder
3   <u>a teaspoon</u> of sugar
4   <u>2</u> eggs
5   <u>30 grams</u> of butter
6   <u>300 ml</u> (millilitres) of milk

3

1   <u>melt</u> some butter
2   <u>mix</u> them altogether
3   <u>heat</u> a pan
4   <u>put</u> a little bit of butter in
5   <u>wait</u> for bubbles to form on the top of the mixture
6   <u>flip</u> the pancake over

(C)

1

    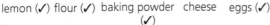

Spice ✓   Cheese   Meat ✓

Chocolate   Beans ✓   Vegetables ✓

2

1   F   2   F   3   T   4   F   5   F

3

1   There's a real depth of <u>flavour</u> there.
2   It has to be very <u>fresh</u> ingredients, a lot of bright
    <u>tastes</u>.
3   There are <u>spices</u> there but it's not about fire.
4   It's very <u>veggie</u>-heavy.
5   It kind of <u>goes with</u> a little bit of everything.

Unit 17 Games and sports

A

1

2

a

	plays twice a week	likes watching	plays with friends	played from age 4 or 5
soccer				✓
golf	✓			
squash			✓	
baseball		✓		

B

1

1 a   2 b   3 b   4 b   5 b

2

1 playing 2 interact 3 go 4 being 5 like

C

1

1 a   2 c   3 c   4 b

2

1 There's a place in rugby for every kind of <u>player</u>.

2 Tall, <u>thin</u> players; small, <u>fat</u> players …

3 It means that you get a great <u>variety</u> of people who enjoy the sport.

4 The 'Six Nations' rugby tournament is an annual tournament.

5 Teams from England, <u>Ireland</u>, Scotland, Wales, <u>France</u>.

6 and, most recently joined, <u>Italy</u>.

	Hazel	Tim
I like playing in a team	✓	
working towards the same goal	✓	
together as a team		✓
you get a great variety of, people who enjoy the sport		✓
it's nice to interact with a team	✓	
come together, in order to win a match		✓

Unit 18 Music and films

A

1

B

1

Why Kerry likes blockbuster movies

not about everyday life
fun
glamourous

Why Kara likes smaller films

interesting stories
good acting
actors earn a sensible amount of money

2

1 F   2 F   3 T   4 F   5 T

3

1 d 2 f 3 b 4 a 5 c 6 e

C

1

1 swing music   3 jazz music   5 Jump Blues
2 dance music   4 big band   6 Rock 'n' roll

2

1 a 2 b 3 c 4 a 5 c 6 b 7 b

3

rocking   brilliant ✓
amazing ✓   fantastic ✓
superb   absolutely fantastic ✓
very hip ✓   great ✓
marvellous   really cool
unbelievably good ✓   absolutely wonderful ✓

4

| 1 N | 2 N | 3 G | 4 N | 5 G | 6 N |

5

| 1 T | 2 F | 3 T | 4 T | 5 F |

Unit 19   Travel and tourism

Ⓐ

1

2 … 3 … 4 … 1 … 6 … 5

2

1	America	5	Sahara Desert	9	Paris
2	Spain	6	Santorini	10	Budapest
3	Mozambique	7	Hong Kong		
4	Argentina	8	London		

Ⓑ

1

| 1 T | 2 T | 3 F | 4 T | 5 F | 6 T |

2

| 1 b | 2 e | 3 f | 4 a | 5 c | 6 d |

Ⓒ

1

1 b

2

| 1 | holiday | 3 | beach (x2) | 5 | sightseeing |
| 2 | day | 4 | weekends | 6 | off |

3

	to relax	to lie on a beach	week-ends away	sight-seeing	different activities	to read a book	to get a tan
likes	✓	✓				✓	✓
quite likes			✓	✓	✓		

Unit 20   Shopping

Ⓐ

1

3 … 4 … 2 … 1 … 5

2

| 1 | holidays | 3 | music | 5 | clothes |
| 2 | books | 4 | groceries | | |

Ⓑ

1

| 1 a | 2 c | 3 a | 4 b | 5 a |

2

| 1 | exhausting | 3 | crowded | 5 | big |
| 2 | fussy; careful | 4 | obvious | | |

Ⓒ

1

| 1 a | 2 b | 3 b | 4 c | 5 b | 6 a |

2

| 1 | high street | 3 | time | 5 | occasionally |
| 2 | online | 4 | try on | 6 | changing room |

3

online: takes less time, free delivery, try clothes at home

high street: more personal experience, safer, customer service, more fun, busy

TRANSCRIPT

The transcript below is an exact representation of what each speaker on the *Listening* CD says. No corrections or adaptations have been made.

Unit 1   Family life

Track 01

Example: I've got two younger sisters.

1   I have two brothers and one sister; and they're all younger than me.

2   I've got two sisters. I'm the youngest.

3   I have a twin sister, and an older brother and sister who are also <u>twins</u>.

4   I have one brother and one sister, and there's quite a big <u>age gap</u>. My brother's fourteen years older than me and my sister's ten years older than me.

5   Um, I've got one sister— younger sister. Um, yes— so just one, there's— there's just two of us, me and my sister.

Track 02

My family are quite spread out as we're all grown up and left home now. Um, but I live quite <u>close</u> to my brother— he lives in London as well. And my older sister, she lives in Salisbury so the three of us are quite close but my <u>twin</u> sister lives in Durham so she's several hours away on the train so I don't see her very much at the moment um … but uh … yeah, we try and meet up when we can, especially Christmas and Easter. So … um … holiday times, really. And … um … we— we still like to play sport together occasionally. When we meet up we'll play tennis or— or squash and … um … hockey <u>in particular</u>, really. This— this summer the— the four of us are meeting up for a hockey tournament in Boscombe. Um, yeah, we try and make excuses to to meet up still.

Track 03

My mum lives in the north of England … um … and I live in London now, so … um … I don't see her very often. Um, my dad … he lives the <u>furthest</u> away. He lives in India. Um, and I see him once a year. Um, I've got— Yeah, I said I have two sisters. Um, so my older sister … she lives in the north as well. She lives quite near my mum. Um, and … uh … she has two children. Um, she's quite funny. She makes me laugh— and she's— she's really clever and she works very hard.

Um, we get on really well. She's training to be a teacher at the moment. Um, she's going to be a … religious education teacher. Um, she— she works at a school quite close to her house. Um, I suppose in terms of <u>personality</u> we're quite similar because … um … we both like teaching and … um … I used to be a teacher. She— Also, she's quite <u>talkative</u>, like me. Um, I think I talk the most, though. Um … and she's … um … very interested in languages. I— I studied Spanish at university and she speaks Italian.

Unit 2   Daily life

Track 04

1   I usually get up at about eight o'clock.

2   I get up in the morning at 6.30.

3   I normally get up at six forty-five in the morning.

4   I usually wake up about seven fifteen and get up about seven thirty.

5   Sometimes I have to work at night, and when I get up at night, I get up at about five o'clock in the evening.

Track 05

Usually the first thing I would do is put the kettle on to make a cup of coffee. And then I would jump in the shower, have a <u>shave</u>, uh … sometimes I eat breakfast. But if I'm <u>running late</u>, which <u>is usually the case</u>, I would <u>skip</u> breakfast … and then just head out toward the train station.

It takes about forty-five minutes to get to work. And then … uh … I check my email and get started for the day.

Track 06

I normally get up at six forty-five in the morning. I then have my breakfast and get dressed and leave for work. I catch the train. And I normally get to work at about eight thirty, where I work in a <u>clinic</u> and also in a hospital. I come home from work at about four thirty and I get back and I cook my dinner, and maybe go out for a <u>walk</u> or watch some TV. And I go to bed at about eleven.

Track 07

I'm a <u>journalist</u> on a morning TV <u>programme</u>, so sometimes I have to work at night. And when I get up at night, I get up at about five o'clock in the evening. And I make my dinner. And then I watch some TV and I have a shower and I go to work. And I work until nine o'clock the next morning, so I work all through the night. And then I come home, I have a bit of breakfast, and I go back to bed.

Unit 3   My childhood

Track 08

1   I was brought up in the countryside … um … so we had a— a really big garden and one summer my brothers and sisters and I built a fantastic tree house.

2   When I was five years old I learned to ride a bike and my dad, every weekend, would take me round the block on it.

3   One of the things I remember from my childhood was … um … when— was when we had our pocket money and then myself and my brother would go to the sweet shop and we would spend our 50 pence each and we would be able to get bags and bags of sweets.

4   The house I grew up in was on the same street as the library so after school and at the weekends I used to spend all my time reading in the library.

5   Uh, during my childhood I spent every weekend at the beach because my grandparents lived there.

Track 09

I grew up in the countryside … um … in the— kind of the <u>middle</u> of North Carolina which is on the east coast of the United States. Um, and yeah, it was— it was a great life actually, growing up in the countryside. Um, when I was a kid, I spent most of my time outside … uh … in the woods, camping, hiking, hunting, various things, fishing. Um, I think I had my first— you know, I had my own fishing <u>gear</u> and my own, kind of, pellet gun, and all my own camping gear probably by the age of ten. Um, and we were— it was our escape … uh … as— as children to get away from our parents for the weekend, we would go camping in the woods all weekend, and, everyone was perfectly OK with that. That's normal where I come from and I think your parents are quite happy to see you off for the weekend and as— as a— as a child it's— it's brilliant to have your independence, even if it is in the— the middle of the woods. Um … but yeah, we … uh … we— we had a lot of interesting <u>wildlife</u> there. Um, so I spent most of my childhood trying to catch snakes and ... uh ... crayfish and various <u>creatures</u> that live in the woods. Uh, so it was— it was a colourful childhood. Quite a contrast I think to people who live in the city. Um, for me it's— even today it's interesting when I think of people who put so much effort into making a camping trip for the weekend or something. And I know that just as a— as a twelve-year-old boy I could pack a backpack and— and <u>survive</u> all weekend in the woods on very little. Um, so yeah, so, it was a very different kind of life than I think most people are used to, but ... uh ... it was a healthy lifestyle and ... uh ... yeah, I hope that if I have kids one day that they'll have the same opportunity.

Track 10

I grew up in Hong Kong. Um, it's a big city, Hong Kong, and I've always liked cities. Um, we lived in a little house – a <u>bungalow</u> – so it had no <u>upstairs</u> and just a <u>downstairs</u>. And it was on the <u>edge</u> of the city and had a little garden which is quite unusual for Hong Kong because most of Hong Kong is lots of big flats. Um, I really loved it. The weather was just beautiful so because it was warm you were outside most of the year, just playing in the garden and things.

Um, we had lots of friends there, and ... um ... I'm from a big family – I'm one of six children – so there was always— there were always children to play with and we were always outside swinging on swings or playing in the garden. Um, I liked going into the city too. Hong Kong's got so many wonderful markets and that's where we used to do all our shopping for food or clothes – just to walk around the markets and look at all the vegetables and choose the different fish and things for <u>dinner</u>. It was a lovely life. I really enjoyed it.

Unit 4   Life changes

Track 11

1   I got my first job in London about five years ago and that was probably the biggest life-changing job so far.

2   My life changed greatly when I had children— Uh, so I have now one son who is eight years old and ... uh ... one daughter who is four years— years old.

3   At the moment I'm single but my life is going to change very soon because I'm getting married in the next few months.

4   I recently moved out of my parents' house ... uh ... to the city so it was a big change, ... um ... but it's made me much more independent.

5   I used to live in New York but two years ago I moved to England, to London, so that was a major life change – but for the better.

Track 12

Well, before I had children ... um ... my work was everything to me. I loved what I did and ... um ... threw every spare moment I had into my work, really. When I had the children, although my work was still very important to me and I was travelling a lot and ... um ... still was furthering my <u>career</u>, I think my priorities changed and I started to see things in a different way. And ... um ... as they've grown up it's been difficult to <u>juggle</u> and balance out work and home life. Um, and where I used to be perhaps more concerned with ... um ... the hours that I was spending in the office and all that kind of thing, I think now I try to put things in balance and ... um ... not take things too seriously, and not to let things just ... uh ... get out of perspective.

Track 13

About ... um ... five or six years ago, I was a <u>lawyer</u>. Um, I found the job a lot of hard work and it was very stressful and it took up a lot of my time over the weekends as well as late evening hours during the week, and I wanted to make a <u>change</u>. So ... um ... I did a course in painting and I did a course in writing. And I started to enjoy it and I started to write books part time while I was working in law, so I'd find some time on a Saturday or something. Um, and then I found I enjoyed it more and more and in the end I decided to leave law. And … um … I went back to university and started an art degree and started writing more and more. And now I write books for children and I'm really pleased that I made the change. I enjoy the work a lot more. It's a lot more creative. Um, I'm my own <u>boss</u> … and I work in the way that I like working— so for me it's been a really successful change.

Unit 5   Your friends

Track 14

Genevieve	Yeah, friends are very important to me. Um, I've had different friends as I've grown up. So I started off with my primary school and secondary school friends that I don't see as often now as I do … um … my <u>current</u> friends from uni. Um, they're— yeah— so important to me. Um, it just it'd be a very lonely— lonely world if you didn't have someone outside of your family to … um … communicate with.
Fliss	Um, I have one sort of best— best friend that I've had since I was in primary school, actually. Um … we went through a stage— we were really close growing up, we went to secondary school together, and then we went to uni, we didn't talk very much at all. And I think it was about four years that we were still— we were still close and we'd talk now and then, but it was difficult because we were sort of located in opposite ends of the country, so that was quite a hard time. When you go to uni you meet a lot of people. And people kind of come and go in your lives, but there are always certain people that stay.
Jeremy	So, I'm an <u>expatriate</u> here so I've got a huge network of friends all over the world. Um, I have friends from America, from California, who are my great friends and I'll always keep in touch with them but I just talk to them really online nowadays. Then I have my friends who live in London and they're really— they're guys I see on the weekend really so … Um, but I also have friends who I live with— who are my housemates— who— I didn't know them before I moved in with them, but they're all international as well, so from France and Spain and Poland. Um, well, without friends I think I'd go crazy. I just wouldn't know to do with myself or my time. So it's good to have people you can relate to and catch up with and express your views and …
Catherine	My friends are very important to me but some of my friends live quite far away from me now – even in different countries – so I don't see them very often. But when we do see each other, it's like no time has passed.
Laura	I feel very lucky to have such a wonderful group of girlfriends. You know, on the weekends we enjoy hanging out at the beach and getting together for barbecues.
Chris	I try to spend time with friends … um … because I think it's important to keep in contact … but I'm often busy at work so I use social media like Facebook and Twitter. Um modern technology's really good for that, I think. Um I Skype and Tweet a lot, really— I actually have an old best friend who … um … lives a long way away but I Skype him at least twice a week.

Track 15

The <u>weirdest</u> thing about moving to— to London was leaving my friends behind. Um, so I— I try and keep in— try and keep up— try and keep in touch with them as much as possible. Um, even to the fact that … uh … they— they visit quite a lot. Uh, sorry, they visit quite a lot. They— they come and use my <u>couch</u> and I use their couch – whenever. Um, I text them once in a while. Um, it's— well— it's not too expensive to— to call them, but … uh … I— I think it's nicer, whenever I land in Dublin, … um … I— I basically just drop into my friends … um … to surprise them. Maybe nine o'clock in the morning— maybe seven o'clock in the morning.

Um, but it's just nice to catch up with people without Facebook sometimes. 'Cause with Facebook you kinda know everything about them, but not … um … you don't know anything. Um … so I— I— I spend a lot of time with them … um … and normally … uh … just go to some— some— some gigs. Um … just eat a lot of food, hang out, that's it.

Yeah, since I've moved to London, … um … I've— I've got— I've found a lot of international friends as well. Um … so I'm— I'm friends with … uh … a lot of Spanish people. Uh, French, Spanish, Italian, American … Uh, like, less Irish people than I've ever been surrounded with before, and … um … I mean, to be honest … uh … with— with— with modern technology … uh … you spend a lot of time with your iPhone and Whatsapp and … uh … Twitter and Facebook and emails, and … uh … basically it's— it's a lot easier to— to keep in contact with people.

Track 16

Hannah	OK so, Hol, what do you think, like, the ingredients for a really good friendship, like, are?
Holly	Um, I think honesty is really important. What do you think?
Hannah	Yeah, I think that's true because … I'm just thinking, there's a lot of times, before I leave the house, where I'll go up to your room, just to get your opinion on what I'm wearing. Because I know, especially if it's a <u>special occasion</u>, then you'll definitely be honest with me, [yeah] even if— even if I don't want to hear it.
Holly	Yeah, but I wouldn't want you to go out of the house in something that I didn't think you'd be comfortable in, and—
Hannah	Yeah exactly, no, and that's what's really good about having such a close friend – is because you can be honest with me and I won't <u>begrudge</u> you for it.
Holly	Yeah, so I'm the same as well. I know that I can trust you and I can trust your opinion, and I think that's really important.
Hannah	Yeah, and I think that's often why I'll listen to your advice as well – because you know me really well …
Hannah	… and therefore it's sort of more difficult to trust them because they don't know me as well. So I think that's something that really comes with time.
Holly	Yeah, I— I agree. And I think being able to give advice and— and listen as well at the same time is important.
Hannah	That's true, yeah, you're a really good listener.
Holly	I think I— I go to you for advice a lot because I know I can trust you and— and hopefully I can give you useful advice as well.
Hannah	Yeah, you do.
Holly	So, I think that's really important …
Holly	… Um, what else?
Hannah	Um, well I think something that's particular to us is, because we live together, it's sort of important we— we make time for each other but we also make time for ourselves because it's— it can be very, I suppose, like, <u>tempting</u> to always go and, like, knock on your door as soon as I get in. But sometimes I know that you'll just want time just to read a book or to speak to someone on the phone and I think because we've lived together now for quite a long time, then we're very good at judging when you might want your own space and when you might want to spend time with friends. And so I think that's something that we're pretty good at now.
Holly	Yeah, I agree, I think that's true. I think it's easy to try and do everything together and if I'm seeing another friend, I would love to invite you along, but I know it is important not to be on top of each other all the time.
Hannah	Yeah. Not to always be a pair.
Holly	Yeah … um … I think that's— I think that's a really good— a good point.

Unit 6   Your house

Track 17

1   I live in an apartment with my husband. It's just us, no pets, no other family, just us.
2   Uh, I live with my wife and our two children, and our three chickens.
3   So there's three people in my flat. There's me, my husband and my three-year-old son.
4   I live in a house with my partner and my two children.
5   I share a house with three other people. My flatmates are two French girls and a girl from England.

Track 18

I live in a really nice terraced house with two other girls. I find the biggest challenge in shared living would probably be the distribution of chores. Cleaning up the kitchen, doing the cleaning generally, the washing machine, hanging the washing out— I think when you're living with people you don't know or you've just met— you have different backgrounds, different cultures— I think the best way to deal with that is communication. The best points about living with other people would be making new friends. Um, just having people around when you just want to hang out, have a chat, someone to come home to. And … uh … yeah, I think the friendship aspect of it – they have friends, you have friends – it kind of brings two big circles together.

Track 19

I do the cooking, and he does the washing-up afterwards, but when it comes to cleaning we disagree on how to clean the house. When we were living together for two years, I realised that he'd only cleaned the bathroom once, and I said it wasn't acceptable, so I made us get a cleaner, and now we don't argue about the cleaning anymore.

Unit 7   Life in the city

Track 20

I like living in Manchester because it's a small city and you can walk everywhere. There's lots of stuff to do. And there are lots of art exhibitions and lots of things on at the cinema. The worst thing about Manchester is there's very little green space. There aren't very many parks near where I live. And if I want to go and sit in the sunshine, I have to get on the train.

Track 21

Yeah, London is just incredible. I mean, the weather's not that great … um … uh … the weather's awful! But the people are fantastic and there's always something happening.

Track 22

I think that what I like most about living in town— living in the city is the ability to explore things very easily. I like going to new coffee shops and new restaurants. And it's easy to meet my friends and to meet new people. I think one of the things I dislike most about living in town is the noise. And I don't like the cost of life in the city … and also, it's very busy.

Track 23

Living in a big city, there's lots to do on any one day. So maybe on a typical day off I would get up and I would go to the corner shop to buy my breakfast, because I don't need to plan ahead. And then I would— Um, when I've had my breakfast I could go to my local part of town and go to the market there, which is a really <u>vibrant</u> market with lots of clothes and … uh … <u>kitchenware</u> and … uh … fresh fish, and everything there: mobile phones; anything you could want. I could wander round there. Then in the afternoon I might … um … meet some friends for lunch and then I might go to a museum. Or I might have a wander in one of the beautiful parks that London has. That's a real positive of London – it has some beautiful parks.

Unit 8   Life in the countryside

Track 24

1   When I think of the countryside I think of animals: sheep and cows.
2   When I think of the countryside I think of beautiful rivers and peace and quiet.
3   When I think of the countryside I think of— there's no cars … um … no pollution.
4   I think about horses in a field because that's what I saw from my window when I was growing up.
5   I think of long country lanes with flowers and wildlife.

Track 25

I'm from the country originally and often go back to my home town in the New Forest. I think what I like about it is that it's quieter and the air's really clean. There are beautiful views and I live near the <u>coast</u>. So I really like being able to go to the sea and see a <u>horizon</u>. The people are friendly … Um, there's less to do in the evenings but more to do during the day. I like outdoor activities like hiking and horse-riding so it's the <u>ideal</u> place to go, and going home feels like going on holiday sometimes.

Track 26

I'm from a seaside town called Teignmouth in Devon. I was born in Teignmouth, I went to school— um … grew up there— lived there for eighteen years. Um, Teignmouth is a <u>typically</u> English seaside town … um … so you have the beach, you have a river, you have the countryside. Um, it's maybe 20,000 people. Um … and it's a great place to grow up. But when you grow up you want to leave! So it's— it's got a slow <u>rhythm</u> and it comes alive in summer a bit more because you get people that come on holiday. They stay in hotels and <u>guest houses</u>, and the fair comes to town and there's the— there's the <u>fiesta</u> in the <u>harbour</u>. But most of the time you know what life is like in Teignmouth, but … uh … It's very pretty and I think when you go back to visit now and when you're older you appreciate just how pretty it is, and what a nice town.

Track 27

I think when you live in a city you really <u>miss</u> the— you miss nature. When I was a child you— you know, I took it for granted that when I woke up every morning you'd see the sea, and you'd see trees and you'd see birds, or you'd hear birds. Um, but you don't see that every day when you live in London – when you live in the city – but it makes you appreciate it more. I mean, yes, there are parks. Yes, there are lots of trees in London. But when you live in— when you grow up in the countryside or on the coast you're <u>surrounded by</u> it more. So yeah, I think that's what I miss.

Unit 9   Living in another country

Track 28

1   I lived in Japan for a year as part of my university degree.
2   I was born in London … um … but when I was … uh … six years old my parents moved to Hong Kong. And so from the age of six to sixteen – so for ten years – I lived in Hong Kong.

3   I lived and worked in Argentina for six months just before I went to university.

4   I moved to Germany when I was about two years old with my family ... um ... and I lived there until I was about seven ... uh ... when I was sent to boarding school in the UK.

5   I was born in Sydney and then moved to London about five years ago now.

Track 29

When I was seventeen years old ... um ... I left New Zealand and went to Austria which is ... um ... about a 36-hour flight away. And I lived there with a family for one year ... uh ... and I went to school there and this has changed my life completely. Um ... because I learned to speak another language ... um ... and I got to know another culture and I think this has changed ... um ... what has happened in my life and it— my life would be very different if I didn't ... uh ... go away to Austria when I was seventeen. I lived with ... um ... a family— with a mum and a dad and I had a host brother and sister who were eight and ten years old when I was there. And I lived in a very small village with only 620 people. Uh, so it was very different to what I was used to in Wellington. Um, and the people in the village were very friendly and welcoming. There were lots of festivals on all the time, and I didn't get very homesick because everybody was so warm and friendly.

Track 30

A lot of British students between finishing what they call their A levels and moving to university do ... um ... something called a gap year where they often work to ... um ... earn enough money and then sometimes they go travelling. So for my gap year ... uh ... I went to Japan and and I stayed with a Japanese family who were friends of friends. Um, and I lived with them and I knew that when I was out there I would be able to teach English and so I'd be able to earn enough money to survive. So, before I went out I worked at a company to earn enough money to pay for the flight. And then when— once I was out there I was able to ... um ... earn money teaching English. Um, it— For me it was ... um ... the first time I'd been away from my family for a long period of time. So I was eighteen and I was away for a whole year and I was living with a Japanese family who were very different from my family and it really ... um ... opened my eyes ... um ... to the differences between Japanese culture – and also made me look at English culture and ...

Track 31

It allowed me to look in depth in— into Japanese culture and also English culture. And made me think about who I am and my identity and why I do things. And it ... um ... really also made me appreciate my family because I found the family that I lived with quite— a little bit difficult. Um, they were very, very strict and they didn't allow their ... um ... children – they had two children of their own, a boy and a girl – and they didn't allow them much freedom or independence whereas my parents ... um ... allowed my sister and I much more independence and I think ... um ... overall I think that's a good thing. And so it made me appreciate my family and family life a lot more.

Unit 10   Getting around

Track 32

1   Excuse me, is the Apollo theatre ... uh ... around here?

2   Excuse me, where is the closest movie theatre here? / Oh, you mean the cinema?

3   Hey, excuse me ... um ... do you know where the hospital is?

4   Excuse me, I'm meeting a friend at the hotel. Uh, which way is it from here?

5   Excuse me ... uh ... I'm trying to get to the sports grounds. How do I get there?

Track 33

1 walk for about five minutes
2 take the first right
3 over the bridge
4 past the park

5 on the left hand corner
6 go straight down this road
7 T-junction
8 carry on north

Track 34

1 Excuse me, is the Apollo Theatre, … uh … around here?

Uh yeah, it is. It's— if you carry on north up this road about seven hundred metres and then it's on the left hand corner when you reach the T-junction.

OK, great, thank you very much.

Any time.

2 Excuse me, where is the closest movie theatre here?

Oh, you mean the cinema?

Uh, yes— yes.

Right, you go up this road here, [uh huh] past the park, [uh huh] take the first left, [OK] then your ri— take the first right and it's on the left. And it's called Riverside Studios.

Perfect, thank you very much.

You're welcome.

3 Hey, excuse me … um … do you know where the hospital is?

Oh, yeah, sure, you just go straight down this road for— walk for about five minutes, and then it's on the right. It's a really big grey building – you can't miss it.

OK, great, thank you very much.

You're welcome.

4 Excuse me, I'm meeting a friend at the hotel. Uh, which way is it from here?

OK, if you … um … walk to the end of the road [uh huh] and take a right, [yep] and it's— it'll be on your left. [OK] You need to find a road called Shortlands.

OK, perfect. Thank you very much.

No problem.

5 Excuse me … uh … I'm trying to get to the sports grounds. How do I get there?

OK, you're quite a bit— distance— You're gonna, … um … have to head back to the bus station [OK] and possibly get a bus directly from there. It's over the bridge, [OK] so be— then it'll be on your right-hand side.

Track 35

[*phone rings*]

Lorna   Hello?

Shawn   Hey, how you doing?

Lorna   Shawn, hi! Have you arrived?

Shawn   I have— I have. I just … uh … I got through <u>customs</u>, … uh … and passport control. I'm, … uh … just, … uh … standing here in the middle of the airport. Just … uh … I just need some directions to your house.

Lorna   Fantastic, fantastic. Oh, it's really easy to get to my place. Um, so, if you come out of customs … uh … and you've got your bag and everything— the tube— uh … if you head for the tube stop, … um … you'll see signs for the underground and it'll take you down to Heathrow tube stop … uh … down to the Piccadilly line. [OK] Um, can— can— can you see them? Just now, at the side …

Shawn	Yeah, I— I— I see the tube. Uh … I— I— I see the tube stops right in front of me. So I'm gonna— I'm gonna take that down right now. Then— and then, once I'm down there, where do I go?
Lorna	Um, so there's only one line, because Heathrow is the— the last stop. So if you take the Piccadilly line, it's the dark blue line … uh … [OK] eastbound, that— that'll take you, … um … towards— towards me. Uh, you don't have to <u>change</u>. [OK] It's just— it's just, you just sit on the train for about half an hour and it'll take you to Hammersmith – that's my stop. [OK] Um, and then when you get to Hammersmith, the tube station is in a shopping centre, so if you take the exit marked for the bus station, you— [OK] you won't actually have to— you— I don't know— Do you have a lot of <u>luggage</u> with you?
Shawn	No, no, I just have … uh … two backpacks, so I'm gonna— I'd <u>rather</u> walk.
Lorna	OK, that, that's fine … um … but take the— the exit for the bus station anyway because that's the right exit. And then [OK] you'll come out into the shopping centre. [OK] Uh, if you pass the supermarket, it should be on your left, … um … and that'll take you out the right exit of the shopping centre. [OK] Um, when— when you get out of the shopping centre, … uh … you come to Fulham Palace Road. [Yep] Um, and that's the main road in— in my area of Hammersmith. You just walk straight down that road. [OK] Um, so, … uh … it's about, … uh … I think maybe a ten minute walk. You probably walk quite quickly, so it'll be ten minutes at the most.
Shawn	Yeah, it shouldn't be a problem.
Lorna	Um, OK, great. Uh, you'll pass a park on your right, [uh huh] and then … um … after about five minutes you'll see a huge, big <u>concrete</u> building – that's the hospital – it's called Charing Cross Hospital – on your left. [OK] Um, then my— my house is about— about two or three minutes' walk from there. Uh, it's called Ellaline Road. It's, [OK] I think it's about four streets after the hospital and it's on the right-hand side. [OK] And my— my house is— it's the second one from the end. It's got a— a blue door. Um, [OK] but if you— if you want, you can just call me when— when you get there.
Shawn	Yeah, definitely. So, just to <u>confirm</u>, [OK] … um … I'm gonna take the Piccadilly line all the way to— to … uh … Hammersmith, get off at Hammersmith, … um … go through the mall, take the bus exit, … uh … don't get on the bus – <u>obviously</u>, 'cause I wanna walk – walk all the way down for about ten minutes … um … four streets after the hospital make a right … um … on the … uh … on the road— on the— on the street, and yours is second from the end, … um … with, on the left, you said, with a blue door? On the— or on the right?
Lorna	It's on the left.
Shawn	On the left, so second house [yep] from the end on the left with a blue door. And … um …, [yep] I'll give you a call when I'm outside.
Lorna	OK, great, fantastic. I can't wait to see you, uh …
Shawn	Perfect, me neither.
Lorna	Have a safe— safe trip, OK? Bye.
Shawn	Thanks, I'll see you soon. [bye] OK, bye. [Bye]

Unit 11   Studying and learning

Track 36

1 I studied music at university.

2 I … um … I did a degree – a double major – in English and Biology.

3 Um, I studied English, … um … at university and I really enjoyed it.

4 Uh, I went to Argentina for a year, to study at the university in Buenos Aires.

5 I studied at the University of Exeter. Um, I did two degrees there – my— my first was a BA in <u>Theology</u>.

Track 37

I recently completed my MBA, which stands for <u>Masters</u> of Business Administration. When I was doing my MBA, I attended full time for about one year at the University of Oxford, in England. You could do an MBA, ... um ... I think pretty much anywhere in the world. Uh, most universities offer the MBA as a two-year course, ... um ... although the one I did was twelve months. I think the work is extremely <u>demanding</u>, especially if you do a shorter one-year course. Um, then the amount of work is very stressful and it is <u>graded</u> very <u>harshly</u>. However, it is also, for some, a— sort of a <u>break</u> from work and a— a chance to learn something new and sort of progress, and a break out of the <u>routine</u> that we all are in. And oftentimes the friendships you form when working so hard can be the most rewarding part, and I am still in touch with my six best friends from business school.

Track 38

I've been playing the guitar for about ten years now, and if someone was wanting to learn, I would recommend just taking some time to learn the chord structures, and then trying to learn some of the— the chords to the music that you like so you can play along with that. I wouldn't really recommend lessons unless you want to get into the more technical side of things, or play really complicated things. I think it's more fun <u>initially</u> to just learn the basics and try to play along with what you like. And you could even get together with some of your friends playing different instruments and— and try to cover some of your favourite music. You should learn probably about six or seven chords, and that's probably enough for most popular songs. Uh, and then you can combine those in a variety of different ways and— and <u>come up with</u>— with lots of different sounds.

Unit 12   Starting work

Track 39

1

1   What was your first job?

2   How old were you?

3   How much were you paid?

4   How long did you spend there?

5   Did you enjoy it?

Track 40

1   So my first job was— I worked in a factory and I had to pack smoked salmon. I worked there for— I think I only lasted one day, because I really didn't like it. And I did this work when I was about 16. I was still a student and this was a holiday job to earn some extra money. And the money I got was, I think, three pounds fifty an hour – which was minimum wage at the time.

2   My first job I got in High School and I had that job for two years and I worked in a toy store across the street from my High School. It was a very good experience because the people who owned the shop lived down the street from my parents' house and they used to have us round for really big Christmas parties. I think I was paid five dollars and eighty-five cents an hour when I first started.

3   My first job ... um ... was a job I got at the age of seventeen ... um ... I believe I worked in a photographic kiosk— let's say in Durban in South Africa. I was paid ... uh ... cash on a weekly basis ... uh ... every Saturday – it was a— a weekend job ... um ... which I was ... uh ... I was doing to earn some pocket money, really. But it was very interesting. Um, I would process ... um ... uh ... camera film for customers who would come in with their cameras and I would process their film ... um ... and print their photos for them. It was a fun job, and I did enjoy it.

4   My first ever job was when I was sixteen and I worked at a fast food restaurant. Uh, I worked there for the whole summer holidays, ... uh ... which was about ... uh ... 8 weeks and ... uh ... I got to work in all the areas ... uh ... within the restaurant from serving customers, to making chips, to cleaning up the floors. I was paid, I think, three pounds fifty per hour, and I hated the whole job.

5   My first job was when I was sixteen years old and it was as a waitress in an expensive restaurant in the local town. It wasn't a great job because the manager was horrible – he was just so— he shouted all the time and he was always angry. The pay was pretty bad – I think I got about five pounds an hour. But we got tips as well, which was good. And I worked there for I think about a year and half in total.

Track 41

1   What experience do you have that is relevant for this role?
2   What qualifications do you have?
3   Have you worked in a similar job before?
4   And can you tell me what you know about the company already?
5   Are you able to work in the evenings or the weekends?
6   Do you have a valid driving licence?

Track 42

So I'm recruiting at the moment. It's a junior <u>position</u> … uh … within a sales team. And so, I'm looking for somebody who is a good communicator and somebody who gets on with people, and also is <u>willing</u> to learn. So, what I look for in my <u>candidate</u> is somebody who's thought about the company that they're going to work for, so they've done some research. Um, that they are open in their communication and that they can express themselves clearly, … um … that they can demonstrate a willingness to learn. Experience is important when you're employing somebody, but if they're a young <u>graduate</u>, it's not always essential. It's more that they can demonstrate they can learn. When a candidate turns up, first impressions do count, so it's important to think about how you're dressed. Dressing smartly gives a good impression, to smile, … um … a good <u>handshake</u> – a handshake is very important, 'cause it gives a positive impression.

Track 43

Um, looking for a job at the moment is quite difficult … um … because there is a lot of <u>unemployment</u> in this country. Um, I am lucky because I have seven years of <u>work experience</u> which means that I don't need to look for very long in order to get a job. Um, I also have worked in the same <u>sector</u> for a long time which means that I— I have a lot of experience. Um, so if a job comes up in that sector I have a good chance of getting it. Um, and I do all the usual things – I've got … um … an updated CV which I … um … I tailor depending on which job I'm applying for. Um, I have gone to many different agencies … um … and that's the way I've got actually all of my jobs in this sector – through agencies. Um, but there's also a very good website called 'Charityjob' which— basically any job that comes up in a <u>charity</u> that is advertised you'll find on that website. Um, looking for a job can be quite hard … um … it's … um … it's hard to <u>motivate</u> yourself when you don't have structure to your days. Um, so you have to be very disciplined with yourself. You have to make sure that you don't just sleep in and … um … watch daytime TV – you actually make sure that you're applying every single day.

Unit 13   Working from home

Track 44

1   I look after kids after school. Um, they come to my house and I help them with their homework and make them an afternoon snack.
2   I translate technical documents from English into German.
3   I prepare the menus and the food for events and parties. Generally, I work at home but sometimes I have to go out to meet clients.
4   I work at home or— or really I work in a shed in the garden … um … which is where I keep the tools and all the different types of wood that I work with. I make chairs and cupboards and cabinets and things like that.

Track 45

Um, I've been working at— from home for a few years now, and it suits me very well because I've small children, so I have to take them to school. Um, and working from home means I'm nearer to their school and I don't have so much of a long commute into the city. Um, I'm a writer so it's quite easy for me to work from home – I have my computer and I have my study, and I'm set up there. Um, it can be a little bit lonely sometimes. I have to make sure that I make time to have a little walk or maybe just go to the shop and buy something small just to get out of the house sometimes. Um, 'cause you sort of— you feel a bit stuck at your desk otherwise, and you haven't had any fresh air and you haven't said 'hello' to anyone. But often the day goes very quickly because I'm racing through the work to try and get time to pick up the children after school. Um, I find I'm quite productive at home – you have to be quite <u>self-disciplined</u> in that you're the one who makes yourself work. Um, there's no one there telling you what to do, … um … which would be easier sometimes! But I enjoy working at home – I like it.

Track 46

I work in an office Monday to Thursday, and on Fridays I work from home … uh … because I live quite far from my office. It's about an hour's drive, … um … so my company provides <u>remote access</u> so I can connect into the— the network and access all the same files and programs from home that I would be able to if I was in the office which makes it pretty easy to— to keep up with things. It's— It's good 'cause it's a lot more <u>relaxed</u> and … uh … gives you time to go out and do <u>errands</u> and other jobs around the house which you don't always have time for. Although I do miss being able to just go up to someone and ask a question, because you kind of rely on email and phone calls which aren't always as good as just getting someone <u>face to face</u> at their desk and asking them what you need to know.

It can be hard to stay <u>motivated</u>, just because there's a lot more <u>distractions</u> around the house than there would be in the office, so I don't know if I could work from home all the time. I don't think I'd get as much done.

Track 47

Yeah, I think it's quite common for people to work from home now because with the internet it's— it's possible for people to— to work just as <u>effectively</u> when they're not in the office. So I think people are happier to let you work from home, if they know you can access everything you need to. And so much <u>communication</u> is done by email now anyway that quite often, even when I'm in the office I don't always talk to people or <u>interact</u> with people. I'd probably send them an email first. So I think it's … uh … yeah, it's definitely gonna become more common.

Unit 14   Your career

Track 48

I work for a supermarket, and I work in the <u>finance</u> department. So, I've worked there for four years. And, um, I decided to work there because I wanted to work in finance. Um, I work quite a lot of hours. The days are quite long. Um, I've got a team of six people that I <u>look after</u>, so there's quite a lot of stuff that I have to kind of help them with. Um, so it is quite demanding but it's— I quite like it and it's busy all the time, so that's good. So, at some point in the future, I would like to have children, and I think I will continue to do my job, although I might not do it as much as I do at the moment.

Track 49

I used to be … uh … a ma— the manager of a <u>youth hostel</u>, … uh … which is a backpackers hostel. Uh, it was quite a challenging job, in that … um … I had to deal with customers face to face on a daily basis, … um … which sometimes is very pleasant and sometimes is very stressful. Uh, dealing with customers could be quite stressful, because, … uh … a lot of my job as a manager was to deal with their <u>complaints</u>. Um, so I didn't have the pleasure of dealing with the people who were happy all the time, but just the people who requested to speak with the manager … uh … so that they could complain about … uh … whatever issue … uh … was troubling them.

Track 50

Um, I'm not far off retirement now. In fact, I could take a <u>pension</u> now – I'm entitled to— … uh … <u>entitled</u> to one. Um, there— there may not even be any work come September because universities are <u>cutting down</u> on the staff, so it might be a— a forced retirement! But I don't mind really 'cause I think it'll be nice just to have a less <u>hurried</u> life … and to do a few— a little bit more of the things you want rather than the things that you feel you have to do.

Unit 15   Your future

Track 51

Right now, I work … uh … as an IT professional, which means that I fix computers when they don't <u>work</u> … uh … and I go out and— and talk to a lot of people about what they need to do with their computers. Ideally, I would like to move away from London, where I live now. It's a big city with a lot of people, … um … but there's not a lot of nature. What I would like about living in the countryside is probably the clean air … um … and the easy access to nature. Um, I would like to work as a blacksmith, which means that you take … um … <u>metal</u> and make it into tools and different things that you can use. Um, I think it would be very nice to work as a blacksmith because I like creating things with my hands. And when you work on a computer, … um … you can't create anything. You don't get anything that you can touch or feel after you are done with your work. Currently it's— it's very easy to sit by a computer and not do a lot. Um, but if you are creating things out of metal, it would be very physical and I would probably be exhausted at the end of the day. I think I would feel much better if— if I were a blacksmith, because of the general exercise you get, because of how you get a sense of accomplishment when you've created something very beautiful.

Track 52

Right now, I live in Los Angeles and I work in <u>real estate</u> selling <u>residential</u> <u>homes</u>. If I could pick anything to do, I'd love to get paid to travel and basically become a professional travel blogger. I would love to create my own website and be able to share and <u>upload</u> photos and— and share my experiences with other people, and places to go, places to eat. You know, sometimes as a tourist, you get caught up in the hype of, you know, things you've read maybe from one travel book or another, but when you're on travel blogging sites you're hearing from so many different people and their different experiences. Maybe you relate to one person more than another and you go, 'wow, you know what? If she liked it, I know I'm <u>gonna</u> like it.' You know, next summer, I'm already planning a trip with my girlfriends to the Croatian Islands and when I get back from there, I— I just can't wait to post all the photos about the places I've been, the places I ate, you know, the <u>nightlife</u>, the beaches. There are so many things … um … I would love to talk about. And if I could get paid to do that, I can't think of a better job <u>on the planet</u>.

Unit 16   Food

Track 53

1   Favourite food? Uh … would be pasta. I do enjoy pasta. Um, I like pasta and meatballs. Spaghetti and meatballs.

2   My favourite meal is roast chicken because I really enjoy meat, and I enjoy the vegetables and the Yorkshire puddings that come with it.

3   I think my favourite food is fruit … um … because it's really healthy, and … um … my favourite fruit is strawberries.

4   My favourite food is Thai food and particularly curry— red curry from Thailand is my— is my favourite food.

Track 54

On … um … Saturday mornings I make pancake mixture for my children. Um, I make it partly because it reminds me of my own childhood – my mother used to make pancakes for us when we were small and … um … my children love having them. It's quite an easy recipe to— to follow. Um, you just need around 225 grams of plain flour … uh … you need a tablespoon or so of baking powder, a bit of sugar, maybe about a teaspoon. 2 eggs. Um, you have to melt some butter, about 30 grams or so of butter is fine. And 300 ml of milk. And you mix them alltogether until it makes a smooth white mixture. And then … um … you heat a pan, you put a little bit of butter in and you pour maybe two or three tablespoons of mixture in. And then you wait for bubbles to form on the top of the mixture and then you flip the pancake over. Um, my children really love it … um … and they cover their pancakes with maple syrup, or honey, or chocolate spread, or sometimes … um … lemon and sugar. And they— they— they always look forward to Saturdays and they can't wait till I make the pancakes.

Track 55

My favourite food, hands down, is Mexican food and it's so difficult to find it where I live now, the trade-off being that you get amazing Indian food. But, absolutely, Mexican food, when I go back to the U.S. I just gorge on it. I think Mexican food is so good because— people have made the assumption that it's just hot, and it's not. There's a real depth of flavour there. It's usually— It has to be very fresh ingredients, a lot of bright tastes. Um, there are spices there but it's not about fire – it's about depth. Um, oftentimes people think that it's just layers and layers of beans and meat but it's not – it's very veggie-heavy. Um, I like the fact that it's very mobile food and that it kind of goes with a little bit of everything.

Unit 17   Games and sports

Track 56

1   The sport I most enjoy is running. I do quite a few triathlons, but running is my favourite aspect.

2   Well, sports is huge for girls in America. Um, so we grow up from the young age of four and five playing soccer, so that's my favourite sport.

3   Golf is my first love, really. I have enjoyed it for some time, and I try and play … um … twice a week if I can.

4   Squash has become a huge favourite. So, love playing squash, and it's a great way to socialize as well, with friends.

5   Uh, I really love football … uh … and my favourite player is Zinedine Zidane.

6   I think my favourite thing about sports, which is not playing them, but watching them … um … is watching baseball – because traditionally in America girls don't play baseball, but every family has its own allegiance to their, you know, local team. And for me it was the Yankees, and I love rooting for them.

Track 57

At the moment, I play hockey in a hockey team. Um, it tends to be just over the winter because that's when the hockey season, … um … is. But I really enjoy that and I like playing in a team. Um, so I like playing team sports because … um … it's nice to interact with a team and kind of feel like you're all working towards the same— same goal. Um, I did used to be a member of a gym but I found it quite difficult to motivate myself to go. And … um … I kind of prefer being in a team sport because you're kind of exercising without really realising it – you're just sort of having fun in a team sport, so that's why I like playing hockey.

Track 58

Uh, rugby is my favourite sport. And … uh … I think that's because … um … it's a sport which … uh … generates great team spirit. Um, uh … there's … uh … there's a place in rugby for … um … every kind of player. Uh, tall, thin players; small, fat players; fast players; strong players. And, um … uh … it means that you get …

uh … a great variety of … um … of people who enjoy the sport … um … who all come together … um … in order to— to win a— a match … uh … together as a team. I generally … uh … watch the Six Nations every year. The Six Nations, … uh … rugby <u>tournament</u> is an <u>annual</u> tournament that involves teams from … uh … England, Ireland, Scotland, Wales, France and, … uh … most … uh … recently joined, Italy.

Unit 18   Music and films

Track 59

1   I like listening to music where a group of people sing together … um … in … uh … often a church setting.

2   I like war films because … uh … I'm a big fan of history and they— they help to bring it to life.

3   I like dance music. Um, the— I mean, I guess partly I like the social side – going out to clubs with friends and stuff and just getting lost in the music and dancing really till, you know, till the morning.

4   I like … um … horror movies. I like them because they scare me and there's something about them that's really funny as well because they're fake. And there's monsters that jump out at you, and they're good fun to watch with friends.

5   I like music that tells a story … um … has instruments like guitars and violins 'cause … um … they're very natural sounding and passionate and vivid and it seems to me that that's what music's about.

6   I really like films that make me laugh, that are light-hearted and have a bit of romance in.

Track 60

Kerry   I really like blockbuster movies, mainstream movies, because they're really <u>escapist</u>. They're larger than life, they're really fun, and they're just, to me, what the movies are about – Hollywood, <u>glamour</u>, again larger than life, bigger than reality and just, getting away from it all for about two hours.

Kara   I completely disagree with you. I can't stand the big blockbuster films. There's just too much action and it's so predictable. Um, when I go to the movies I wanna be absorbed in a beautiful storyline with really good actors that aren't earning twenty millions dollars. Um, that there's a real core to the movie – a core story.

Kerry   I agree with the core story, I think it's a really good point and really good actors. But I don't think a blockbuster <u>precludes</u> those things. I think that generally once you get to blockbuster level the people who are working on the movie are all so <u>talented</u> and well paid because there's a kind of <u>guarantee</u> that it's gonna be really entertaining at that level.

Kara   Maybe I just hate going to see what everyone else is seeing and everyone else is talking about so I rebel against going to that one movie that's making all the money.

Track 61

Graham   Right now I'm listening to a lot of swing music. It's just amazing. It's very hip at the moment as well. Um, if you listen to a lot of … um … dance music, there's a lot of swing being put in to dance music at— at the moment. Um, yeah the music I listen to first came out in the United States – America – in the 1930s and 40s and had <u>developed</u> from … uh … jazz music in the 1920s. The— the band set-up, typically, might be … um … ten <u>horns</u>, … uh … a drummer, singer— but then there was the— the more underground stuff … uh … in the— in the bars. Um, the 'speakeasies' just have fewer <u>horns</u>, maybe three or four horns, … uh … a drummer, … uh … and a singer.

Well-known names might be … uh … Benny Goodman, Glenn Miller … uh … for the <u>big</u> stuff. And then the small stuff … uh … is some great, great guys – uh … Louis Jordan, just check him out, absolutely fantastic. Uh, Cab Calloway. Brilliant stuff. 'Cause you know <u>big band</u>? It is fantastic, … um … but that's very much the clean side of it. You get into the … uh … the jitterbug stuff, the small bands, 'cause not everyone can afford to have a big band or go to clubs where there were … um … you know, loads of, … um … instruments and stuff so in the small bars, 'Jump Blues' is the sort of like underground version of swing in the 1940s. That is just unbelievably good. And all the Rock 'n' Roll that came out – all your Chuck Berry, Elvis – it is Jump Blues.

Nikki	My boyfriend's really into jazz and everything so …
Graham	Well, jazz— for me— does it— what era does he like? Do you know?
Nikki	Um, he likes …
Graham	Has it got a tune?
Nikki	He— oh— he likes all the kind of … um … Ella Fitzgerald and all that kind of stuff.
Graham	Brilliant, yeah that's the good stuff, 'cause after the Second World War when 'bop' came, it just gets— it loses the dance floor. Uh, the— Ella Fitzgerald is just absolutely wonderful.
Nikki	Yeah, he's really into it. There's a— there's a jazz night that we go to in London Bridge every month that he just adores, and just loses himself in it every night. I like some of it but not the really hardcore stuff that you almost can't feel the rhythm in anymore because it's so all over the place.
Graham	Well there— I mean, that's a great … uh … style of music to play, but not to listen to.

Unit 19   Travel and tourism

Track 62

1   Recently, … um … I went to visit my friend who lives in Mozambique. He lives in the capital, Maputo, … um … not far from the sea.

2   I went to Tunisia about two months ago. Um, we had a really nice camel ride out in the Sahara Desert.

3   My favourite vacation that I took recently was a trip to the Greek Islands. We were there for about ten days and we visited three islands— um, Santorini, Paros and Mykonos.

4   I used to work in export sales, so I travelled a lot to … uh … Thailand, Taiwan, Hong Kong, Japan, and other Asian countries.

5   I recently went to the east coast of America with a friend and had the most amazing time. Uh, my friend and I travelled from Boston, to Washington DC, to New York.

6   Um, I recently went to Budapest with my mother. So we got to walk along the river and go to some bathhouses, and … um … see a castle.

Track 63

In Argentina there's lots of really beautiful landscape. So there's mountains in the south, and … um … really beautiful places to visit. Um, but because it's such a big country, you have to travel quite long distances. You can fly, but it can sometimes be quite expensive. So most people travel by bus … um … because there aren't any trains. Um, so, some of the bus journeys are sixteen or twenty hours long.

Track 64

I like to relax when I'm on holiday, I think because I spend so much of my working day in quite stressful situations, so I do like to just get on a beach and lie on a beach. Um, but I also quite like having weekends away to interesting places, so— you know, European cities or even places in the UK that I've never been to before. I quite like just having a couple of days of city or sightseeing or— or doing different activities, but— no, when I— if I have a week off work, I like to sit on a beach, read a book, get a tan …

Unit 20   Shopping

Track 65

1   I don't have time to go the supermarket, so I buy all my groceries online.

2   I never buy CDs any more. Um, I buy all my music online.

3   I love buying my holidays online – buying the flights and booking the hotels …

4   Um, so I shop for clothes a lot online … um … because when I go into stores I <u>struggle</u> to find … um … clothes in my <u>size</u>.

5   I find it easier to buy books online. I think you can get them delivered very <u>conveniently</u>.

Track 66

One of my favourite things to do is to go shopping for clothes. Um, I like to look round department stores. I often go back several times to look at the same thing. The great thing about department stores is that they have everything in one place, so it's not too exhausting looking round and seeing what you'd like to buy. Um, I probably go shopping once a month. I might not buy something every month but I do like to go and have a look around. I'm really <u>fussy</u> and very careful about what I buy. I tend to go back to the same places, because I really like it when the store is really nicely laid out and it's more of an experience to go shopping. I really hate … um … <u>crowded</u> shops, or where they haven't <u>displayed</u> the things properly. Um, I do like some brands and I'll often buy … um … from the same companies, but I don't like it to be obv— too obvious. I don't like clothes which have got big logos on them or things like that.

Track 67

Genevieve   So, do you prefer high street shopping or online shopping?

Fliss   I like online shopping more. I— <u>don't get me wrong</u> – I do like shopping, in the high street, in Oxford Street, that kind of thing. But I do like online shopping, just because it's easier and I haven't got time to shop all the time. There are certain really good online shops as well, that have free delivery.

Genevieve   I love high street shopping. [*Oh, OK*] I— I think it's more person— uh, personal. Um, you get the <u>customer service</u> and you can try on your clothes before you bring it back.

Fliss   But good customer service, do you get?

Genevieve   Yeah, occasionally bad, but the majority I've experienced is good. [*It's OK*] And I think it's more— it's more personal and you— you <u>get a feel for</u> the clothes and that— I think that whenever I have bought things online, I end up bringing it— bringing it back [*Yeah*] because it doesn't fit or it's not quite right and it doesn't quite look like the picture.

Fliss   But then— but then I just think you get the safety— And you can try it on in your own home and you don't have to be in a <u>squashed</u>, hot changing room, where it's horrible lighting, and—

Genevieve   But that's the fun of it! [*Oh*] I love the busy— the busyness of it. It's fun. I think it's really fun. It's— Yeah, you get that kind of personal experience, and it's— it's just a nice experience.

LIST OF ACCENTS

Below is a list of all of the accents that are used in each unit:

Unit 1   Family life

A Scottish, American, American, English, English, English

B English

C English

Unit 2   Daily life

A New Zealand, English, English, English, English

B English

C English

D English

Unit 3   Childhood

A English, English, English, English, Australian

B American

C English

Unit 4   Life changes

A English, English, American, English, American

B English

C English

Unit 5   Your friends

A English, English, American, English, American, English

B Irish

C English, English

Unit 6   Your house

A American, English, English, American, Scottish

B Australian

C English

Unit 7   Life in the city

A English, Australian

B English

C Scottish

Unit 8   Life in the countryside

A Scottish, English, English, Australian, English

B English

C English, English

Unit 9   Living in another country

A English, English, Scottish, English, Australian

B New Zealand

C English, English

Unit 10   Getting around

A American, English

B Scottish, American

Unit 11   Studying and learning

A Canadian, American, English, English, English

B American

C Northern Irish

Unit 12   Starting work

A English, Canadian, South African, English, Scottish

B English

C English

D English

Unit 13   Working from home

A Australian, Australian, English, English

B English

C Northern Irish

Unit 14   Your career
A   English
B   American
C   English

Unit 15   Your future
A   Swedish
B   American

Unit 16   Food
A   English, English, English, English
B   English
C   American

Unit 17   Games and sports
A   English, American, South African, Australian, English, American
B   English
C   English

Unit 18   Music and films
A   American, English
B   American, American
C   English, Scottish

Unit 19   Travel and tourism
A   English, American, American, English, Welsh, American
B   English
C   English

Unit 20   Shopping
A   English, American, Scottish, English, English
B   English
C   English